D0331712

AN ORDINARY MAN

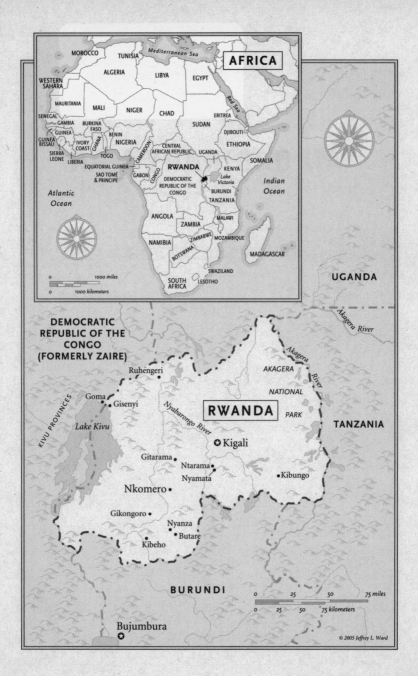

AFRICA

MOROCCO TUNISIA
Mediterranean Sea
WESTERN SAHARA
ALGERIA LIBYA EGYPT
MAURITANIA
MALI NIGER CHAD SUDAN
Red Sea
ERITREA
SENEGAL
GAMBIA BURKINA FASO DJIBOUTI
GUINEA BISSAU GUINEA BENIN NIGERIA CENTRAL AFRICAN REPUBLIC ETHIOPIA
IVORY COAST GHANA TOGO CAMEROON UGANDA SOMALIA
SIERRA LEONE LIBERIA EQUATORIAL GUINEA RWANDA KENYA *Lake Victoria*
SAO TOMÉ & PRINCIPE GABON CONGO DEMOCRATIC REPUBLIC OF THE CONGO BURUNDI *Indian Ocean*
TANZANIA
Atlantic Ocean
ANGOLA ZAMBIA MALAWI
NAMIBIA ZIMBABWE MOZAMBIQUE
BOTSWANA
MADAGASCAR
SWAZILAND
SOUTH AFRICA LESOTHO

0   1000 miles
0   1000 kilometers

UGANDA

DEMOCRATIC REPUBLIC OF THE CONGO (FORMERLY ZAIRE)

Akagera River

Ruhengeri
Goma
Gisenyi
Nyabarongo River
AKAGERA
NATIONAL
PARK
Akagera River
KIVU PROVINCES
Lake Kivu
RWANDA
✪ Kigali
TANZANIA
Gitarama
Ntarama
Nyamata
Kibungo
Nkomero •
Gikongoro •
Nyanza
Butare
Kibeho

BURUNDI

0   25   50   75 miles
0   25   50   75 kilometers

Bujumbura ✪

© 2005 Jeffrey L. Ward

AN ORDINARY MAN

PAUL RUSESABAGINA

with
Tom Zoellner

BLOOMSBURY

First published in Great Britain 2006
This paperback edition published 2007

Copyright © 2006 Paul Rusesabagina

The moral right of the author has been asserted

No part of this book may be used or reproduced in any
manner whatsoever without written permission from the
Publisher except in the case of brief quotations embodied
in critical articles or reviews.

Bloomsbury Publishing Plc,
36 Soho Square,
London W1D 3QY

A CIP catalogue record for this book
is available from the British Library

ISBN 9780747585589

10 9 8 7 6 5 4 3 2 1

Printed and bound in Great Britain
by Clays Ltd, St Ives plc

Bloomsbury Publishing, London, New York and Berlin

All papers used by Bloomsbury Publishing are natural, recyclable products
made from wood grown in well-managed forests. The manufacturing
processes conform to the environmental regulations of the country of origin.

www.bloomsbury.com

To all the victims of the 1994 Rwandan Genocide,
to their widows and orphans, to the survivors.

To Tatiana, my wife and right hand;
to Lys, Roger, Diane and Tresor Rusesabagina
as well as Anaise and Carine Karimba.

ACKNOWLEDGMENTS

The authors wish to thank Kathryn Court, Jill Kneerim, Alexis
Washam, and Paul Buckley for their invaluable assistance in
the production of this book.

"Many fledging moralists in those days were going about our town proclaiming that there was nothing to be done about it and we should bow to the inevitable. And Tarrou, Rieux, and their friends might give one answer or another, but its conclusion was always the same, their certitude that a fight must be put up, in this way or that, and there must be no bowing down. The essential thing was to save the greatest possible number of persons from dying and being doomed to unending separation. And to do this there was only one resource: to fight the plague. There was nothing admirable about this attitude; it was merely logical."

—From *The Plague*, by Albert Camus

AUTHOR'S NOTE

This is a work of nonfiction. All of the people and events described herein are true as I remember them. For legal and ethical reasons, I have given pseudonyms to a handful of private Rwandan citizens. Each time this is done, the change is noted in the text.

Paul Rusesabagina

INTRODUCTION

My name is Paul Rusesabagina. I am a hotel manager. In April 1994, when a wave of mass murder broke out in my country, I was able to hide 1,268 people inside the hotel where I worked.

When the militia and the Army came with orders to kill my guests, I took them into my office, treated them like friends, offered them beer and cognac, and then persuaded them to neglect their task that day. And when they came back, I poured more drinks and kept telling them they should leave in peace once again. It went on like this for seventy-six days. I was not particularly eloquent in these conversations. They were no different from the words I would have used in saner times to order a shipment of pillowcases, for example, or tell the shuttle van driver to pick up a guest at the airport. I still don't understand why those men in the militias didn't just put a bullet in my head and execute every last person in the rooms upstairs but they didn't. None of the refugees in my hotel were killed. Nobody was beaten. Nobody was taken away and made to disappear. People were being hacked to death with machetes all over Rwanda, but that five-story building became a refuge for anyone who could make it to our doors. The hotel could offer only an illusion of safety, but for whatever reason, the illusion prevailed and I survived to tell the story, along with those I sheltered. There was nothing particularly heroic about it. My only pride in the matter is that I stayed at my post and continued to do my job as manager when all other aspects of decent life vanished. I kept the Hotel Mille Collines open, even as the nation descended into chaos and eight hundred thousand people were butchered by their friends, neighbors, and countrymen.

It happened because of racial hatred. Most of the people hiding in my hotel were Tutsis, descendants of what had once been the ruling class of Rwanda. The people who wanted to kill them were mostly Hutus, who were traditionally farmers. The usual stereotype is that Tutsis are tall and thin with delicate noses, and Hutus are short and stocky with wider noses, but most people in Rwanda fit neither description. This divide is mostly artificial, a leftover from history, but people take it very seriously, and the two groups have been living uneasily alongside each other for more than five hundred years.

You might say the divide also lives inside me. I am the son of a Hutu farmer and his Tutsi wife. My family cared not the least bit about this when I was growing up, but since bloodlines are passed through the father in Rwanda, I am technically a Hutu. I married a Tutsi woman, whom I love with a fierce passion, and we had a child of mixed descent together. This type of blended family is typical in Rwanda, even with our long history of racial prejudice. Very often we can't tell each other apart just by looking at one another. But the difference between Hutu and Tutsi means everything in Rwanda. In the late spring and early summer of 1994 it meant the difference between life and death.

Between April 6, when the plane of President Juvenal Habyarimana was shot down with a missile, and July 4, when the Tutsi rebel army captured the capital of Kigali, approximately eight hundred thousand Rwandans were slaughtered. This is a number that cannot be grasped with the rational mind. It is like trying—all at once—to understand that the earth is surrounded by billions of balls of gas just like our sun across a vast blackness. You cannot understand the magnitude. Just try! Eight hundred thousand lives snuffed out in one hundred days. That's eight thousand lives a day. More than five lives per *minute*. Each one of those lives was like a little world in itself. Some person who laughed and cried and ate and thought and felt and hurt just like any other person, just like you and me. A mother's child, every one irreplaceable.

And the way they died . . . I can't bear to think about it for long. Many went slowly from slash wounds, watching their own blood gather in pools in the dirt, perhaps looking at their own severed limbs, oftentimes with the screams of their parents or their children or their husbands in their ears. Their bodies were cast aside like garbage, left to rot in the sun, shoveled into mass graves with bulldozers when it was all over. It was not the largest genocide in the history of the world, but it was the fastest and most efficient.

At the end, the best you can say is that my hotel saved about four hours' worth of people. Take four hours away from one hundred days and you have an idea of just how little I was able to accomplish against the grand design.

What did I have to work with? I had a five-story building. I had a cooler full of drinks. I had a small stack of cash in the safe. And I had a working telephone and I had my tongue. It wasn't much. Anybody with a gun or a machete could have taken these things away from me quite easily. My disappearance—and that of my family—would have barely been noticed in the torrents of blood coursing through Rwanda in those months. Our bodies would have joined the thousands in the east-running rivers floating toward Lake Victoria, their skins turning white with water rot.

I wonder today what exactly it was that allowed me to stop the killing clock for four hours.

There were a few things in my favor, but they do not explain everything. I was a Hutu because my father was Hutu, and this gave me a certain amount of protection against immediate execution. But it was not only Tutsis who were slaughtered in the genocide; it was also the thousands of moderate Hutus who were suspected of sympathizing with or even helping the Tutsi "cockroaches". I was certainly one of these cockroach-lovers. Under the standards of mad extremism at work then I was a prime candidate for a beheading.

Another surface advantage: I had control of a luxury hotel, which was one of the few places during the genocide that had the image of being protected by soldiers. But the important word in that sentence is *image*. In the opening days of the slaughter, the United Nations had left four unarmed soldiers staying at the hotel as guests. This was a symbolic gesture. I was also able to bargain for the service of five Kigali policemen. But I knew these men were like a wall of tissue paper standing between us and a flash flood.

I remembered all too well what had happened at a place called Official Technical School in a suburb called Kicukiro, where nearly two thousand terrified refugees had gathered because there was a small detachment of United Nations soldiers staying there. The refugees thought—and I don't blame them—that the blue helmets of the UN would save them from the mobs and their machetes. But after all the foreign nationals at the school were put onto airplanes safely, the Belgians themselves left the country, leaving behind a huge crowd of refugees begging for protection, even begging to be shot in the head so they wouldn't have to face the machetes. The killing and dismemberment started just minutes later. It would have been better if the soldiers had never been there to offer the illusion of safety. Even the vaguest rumor of rescue had been fatal to those on the wrong side of the racial divide. They had clustered in one spot and made it easy for their executioners to find them. And I knew my hotel could become an abattoir just like that school.

Yet another of my advantages was a very strange one. I knew many of the architects of the genocide and had been friendly with them. It was, in a way, part of my job. I was the general manager of a hotel called the Diplomates, but I was eventually asked to take charge of a sister property, the nearby Hotel Mille Collines, where most of the events described in this book took place. The Mille Collines was *the* place in Kigali where the power classes of Rwanda came to meet Western businessmen and dignitaries. Before the killing started I had shared drinks with most of these men, served them complimentary plates of lobster, lit their cigarettes. I knew the names of their wives and their children. I had stored up a large bank of favors. I cashed them all in—and then borrowed heavily—during the genocide. My preexisting friendship with General Augustin Bizimungu in particular helped save the Mille Collines from being raided many times over. But alliances always shift, particularly in the chaos of war, and I knew my supply of liquor and favors would run dry in some crucial quarters. Before the hundred days were over a squad of soldiers was dispatched to kill me. I survived only after a desperate half hour during which I called in even more favors.

All these things helped me during the genocide. But they don't explain everything.

Let me tell you what I think was the most important thing of all.

I will never forget walking out of my house the first day of the killings. There were people in the streets who I had known for seven years, neighbors of mine who had come over to our place for our regular Sunday cookouts. These people were wearing military uniforms that had been handed out by the militia. They were holding machetes and were trying to get inside the houses of those they knew to be Tutsi, those who had Tutsi relatives, or those who refused to go along with the murders.

There was one man in particular whom I will call Peter, though that is not his real name. He was a truck driver, about thirty years old, with a young wife. The best word I can use to describe him is an American word: *cool.* Peter was just a cool guy; so nice to children, very gentle, kind of a kidder, but never mean with his humor. I saw him that morning wearing a military uniform and holding a machete dripping in blood. Watching this happen in my own neighborhood was like looking up at a blue summer sky and seeing it suddenly turning to purple. The entire world had gone mad around me.

What had caused this to happen? Very simple: words.

The parents of these people had been told over and over again that they were uglier and stupider than the Tutsis. They were told they would never be as physically attractive or as capable of running the affairs of the country. It was a poisonous stream of rhetoric designed to reinforce the power of the elite. When the Hutus came to power they spoke evil words of their own, fanning the old resentments, exciting the hysterical dark places in the heart.

The words put out by radio station announcers were a major cause of the violence. There were explicit exhortations for ordinary citizens to break into the homes of their neighbors and kill them where they stood. Those commands that weren't direct were phrased in code language that everybody understood: "Cut the tall trees. Clean your neighborhood. Do your duty." The names and addresses of targets were read over the air. If a person was able to run away his position and direction of travel were broadcast and the crowd followed the chase over the radio like a sports event.

The avalanche of words celebrating racial supremacy and encouraging people to do their duty created an alternate reality in Rwanda for those three months. It was an atmosphere where the insane was made to seem normal and disagreement with the mob was fatal.

Rwanda was a failure on so many levels. It started as a failure of the European colonists who exploited trivial differences for the sake of a divide-and-rule strategy. It was the failure of Africa to get beyond its ethnic divisions and form true coalition governments. It was a failure of Western democracies to step in and avert the catastrophe when abundant evidence was available. It was a failure of the United States for not calling a genocide by its right name. It was the failure of the United Nations to live up to its commitments as a peacemaking body.

All of these come down to a failure of words. And this is what I want to tell you: Words are the most effective weapons of death in man's arsenal. But they can also be powerful tools of life. They may be the only ones.

Today I am convinced that the only thing that saved those 1,268 people in my hotel was words. Not the liquor, not money, not the UN. Just ordinary words directed against the darkness. They are so important. I used words in many ways during the genocide—to plead, intimidate, coax, cajole, and negotiate. I was slippery and evasive when I needed to be. I acted friendly toward despicable people. I put cartons of champagne into their car trunks. I flattered them shamelessly. I said whatever I thought it would take to keep the people in my hotel from being killed. I had no cause to advance, no ideology to promote beyond that one simple goal. Those words were my connection to a saner world, to life as it ought to be lived.

I am not a politician or a poet. I built my career on words that are plain and ordinary and concerned with everyday details. I am nothing more or less than a hotel manager, trained to negotiate contracts and charged to give shelter to those who need it. My job did not change in the genocide, even though I was thrust into a sea of fire. I only spoke the words that seemed normal and sane to me. I did what I believed to be the ordinary things that an ordinary man would do. I said no to outrageous actions the way I thought that anybody would, and it still mystifies me that so many others could say yes.

ONE

I WAS BORN on the side of a steep hill in the summer of 1954. My father was a farmer, my mother his helper. Our house was made of mud and sticks. We were about a mile away from the nearest village. The first world I can remember was green and bright, full of cooking fires and sisters murmuring and drying sorghum and corn leaves in the wind and the warm arms of my mother.

Our house had three rooms. There were small windows with pieces of hinged wood to keep out the sun and rain. The house was built on an incline of terraced farms, but the small yard outside was flat. My mother kept it swept clean of seed-pods and leaves with a homemade broom made out of bundled twigs. When I grew old enough she would let me help her. I still remember the happiness I felt on the day when she trusted me to do it by myself.

From the courtyard you could look south across the winding Ruvayaga Valley to the opposite hill. It seemed an awesome distance, like looking into another country. The hill was laced, as ours was, with houses made out of mud and stucco and baked red tiles, dots of cattle grazing, the groves of avocado plants, and the paddlewide leaves of the banana trees that practically sparkled in the sun. On a perfect day you could lie in the grass near our home and see people at work in the fields on the next hill. They looked like ants. Every now and then somebody's machete would catch the angle of the sun and you'd see the winking of metal across the valley. And far, far in the distance you could make out the clustered roofs of the village called Gitwe, where my parents told me I would one day learn how to read and write, which neither of them could do.

We spoke the beautiful language of Kinyarwanda, in which I first learned the names of the world's many things in rich deep vowels made in the back of the mouth. Bird, *inyoni*. Mud, *ur-woondo*. Stones, *amabuye*. Milk, *amata*.

To enter our house through the front door you had to step up on a stoop made of gray rocks. It couldn't have been more than two feet off the courtyard, but it seemed like a towering height. I used to climb in on my hands and knees. To the side of the door was a flat stone used for sharpening machetes. There was a shallow depression in the middle where rainwater would collect. After a storm I would splash my hands around in the cool water, putting it on my face and letting it dribble down my cheeks. It was the best part of the rain. When those storms came in September the lightning and thunder scared me. My three younger brothers and I would sometimes huddle together during the worst ones. And then we would laugh at each other for our cowardice. Thunder, *inkuba*.

My parents raised nine children altogether, and I was an island in time's river, separated by six years from my older sister and five years from my younger brother. I got a lot of attention from my mother as a result, and trailed her around the house hoping she would reward me with a chore. The firmament of our relationship was work; we expressed love to one another in the thousands of little daily actions that kept a rural African family together. She showed me how to take care of the baby goats and cows, and how to grind cassava into flour. Even when I came back to visit my parents when I was grown it would be only minutes before I would find myself holding an empty jerrican and going to fetch well water for my mother.

There was a narrow path from the main road that twisted up the side of the ridge and passed through groves of banana trees. I had learned how to walk on this path. It was our connection with a small village called Nkomero, which occupies the top of one of the hundreds of thousands of hills in Rwanda. The nickname for my country is "the land of thousands of hills," or *le pays des mille collines*, but this signifies a gross undercount. There are at least half a million hills, maybe more. If geography creates culture, then the Rwandan mind is shaped like solid green waves. We are the children of the hills, the grassy slopes, the valley roads, the spider patterns of rivers, and the millions of rivulets and crevasses and buckles of earth that ripple across this part of Central Africa like the lines on the tired face of an elder. If you ironed Rwanda flat, goes the joke, it would be ten times as big. In this country we don't talk about coming from a particular *village,* but a particular *hill.* We had to learn the hard way how to arrange our plots of corn and cabbage into flat terraces on the sloping ground so as not to turn a farm into an avalanche. Every inch of arable land is used this way. The daily walk up to a family grove can be an exercise in calf-straining misery going up, and in thigh-wracking caution going down. I think our legs must be the most muscular on the African continent.

There is a story about the conqueror of Mexico, Hernán Cortés, who was asked by the king of Spain to describe the topography of the rugged new nation. Cortés reached for the map on the table and crumpled it up into a ball. "That," he said, "is what Mexico looks like." He could just as easily have been talking about Rwanda. If you didn't grow up here you would be likely to get very, very lost among those seductive hills and valleys.

Our family had rows of sorghum and bananas planted on the slopes of two hills, which made us solidly middle class by the standards of rural Africa in the 1950s. We would have been considered quite poor, of course, when viewed through the lens of a European nation, but it was all we knew and there was always plenty to eat. We worked hard and I grew up without shoes. But we laughed a lot. And I knew there was love in my family before

I knew the word for it.

I think the greatest hero in my life was my father, Thomas Rupfure. He was already an old man, well into his sixties, when I was a child, and he seemed impossibly tall and strong. I could not comprehend that I could one day be his age, or that he was once mine. I assumed he had always been old.

I never once heard him raise his voice. He didn't need to. He always spoke without apology or flourish and with a calm self-possession. If he and my mother ever fought I never knew it. On special days he would fold my hand into his and take me up the winding path to the top of the hill, and then down the rutted road that led to the village, where we would go to buy sweet potatoes or bags of corn. We walked past the houses of our neighbors, and he would greet each one with a gentle nod. Anyone who engaged my father in conversation was likely in for a long story. He loved to talk in proverbs. It was the way he understood the world and his favorite way of dispensing wisdom. Here's an example: Somebody might tell him a story about being taxed at too high a rate by the mayor, and he would start talking about a lamb and a dog drinking out of the same river. The dog accused the lamb of dirtying his water, but the lamb pointed out that that was impossible, since the dog was upstream. The dog then said that the lamb must have dirtied the water yesterday, and the lamb pointed out that that was also impossible, because he had not been in the meadows yesterday. Then it must have been your *brother*!, said the dog, and he proceeded to devour the lamb. The moral of the story was that any excuse will serve a tyrant. I would have cause to remember that tale much later in life.

There was not much to our village of Nkomero, then or today. There is a commune house, which is synonymous with town hall. There is a small Roman Catholic church. There are a few stores that sell bags of sugar, salt, and soft drinks. There is a tavern where men lounge and drink the potent beer made from bananas. A car or a truck coming through was a big event. Behind the wheel, very often, was a white man—a European missionary or a doctor. *Muzungu!* the children would call, a word that means "white man," and they would say it with relish. It was not meant as an insulting word, just a descriptive one, and the white people would smile back at us. We were always hoping for a toss of candy or a ballpoint pen, which would sometimes come and sometimes not.

The road wound past the church and the tavern and on along the ridgetop through a grove of eucalyptus trees on the other side of the Ruvayaga Valley, tracing a long horseshoe shape all the way to the next village, Gitwe. I would walk these two miles literally thousands of times while growing up, so many times that I could practically do it blindfolded, knowing where the road turned just by counting the number of steps I had taken. It was an important symbol in my life, this rutted track that connected my home with my school. It was where I first understood that in order to make progress as a man you had to take a journey. There was only so much you could learn at home before you had to get out in the world and prove what you could do.

It was my father who first took me down this road to the school at Gitwe when I was eight years old, and I still remember him handing me off to the assistant principal and saying good-bye. I suppose it should have been a troubling moment for me—it was the first time I was leaving my parents' care—but I was eager to begin the adventure of learning. My father had told me over and over again: "If you are willing to do it, you will be successful." I was experiencing a privilege he had never had and I know now that he was sending a little piece of himself with me that day.

Perhaps it had something to do with growing up with such a large family, but I found that I could get on well with the new kids in my school. We played soccer, of course, and racing games to see who could run the fastest. Another game was a variation of capture the flag in which the idea was to venture inside enemy territory and grab one of their sticks without being caught.

One strange game I remember in particular was called *igihango,* which is a word loosely translated in English as "trust." There were no clearly defined rules to this game, and I'm not sure you could even call it a game in the classic sense of the word. The idea was that you made a secret agreement to be friends with a particular kid, only you weren't supposed to tell anybody else about it. Other kids tried to make you confess your *igihangos* by holding you down and tickling you or poking you in the ribs or whatever other kind of boyish sadism they could dream up. I was always very good about keeping my *igihango* confidences to myself, at least verbally, but I think I always exposed them when I ran to save one or another of my secret allies from being interrogated. I probably should have been more subtle.

When I went home from school in the evenings I would help my mother cook supper. My brothers and I used hoes to carve out brick-shaped pieces of dirt and we built a kind of domed oven out of them. We stuffed a bunch of sweet potatoes inside and then lit a small fire underneath them. They came out charred and delicious. Every oven was used only once. We kicked it back into the ground, so as to bury the ashes, and then built a new one the next night.

Our suppers always came with small tastes of a bitter and delicious beer made out of the juice of bananas. Let me tell you about this drink, which we call *urwagwa*. Visitors to Rwanda always complain that it tastes like spoiled buttermilk, but I think it is tasty. It plays a central role in Rwandan social life, and is also an important symbol of the good-heartedness and collegiality that I think represents the best side of my country. There is a saying: "You never invite a man without a beer." It is the symbol of hospitality, a way of saying without words, "You are my friend and I can relax in your presence."

Brewing banana beer is like the art of friendship: simple and very complicated at once. First you dig a pit in the earth. Because Rwanda is just a few miles below the equator, the ground temperature is always warm. It acts like a very slow, gentle oven for the fermentation. You take a bunch of ripe bananas, as many as you want, and bury them about four feet deep. You make a lid for the pit out of the broad leaves of the banana tree. Come back in three days and dig them up. They should be very overripe. You transfer the mushy fruit to a basin made out of a hollowed tree trunk and then press down on them using handfuls of tough grass as your gloves. You drain out the juice into a clay pot, strain out the chunks, mix it with sorghum flour as a fermenting agent, let it sit for about a month, and then you have your banana beer.

It is a simple recipe, but it takes years of practice to get it right. You have to feel your way around and make mistakes. This is normal. We have all tasted bad beer. Sometimes the banana juice comes out too light and you have to put it over a fire to reduce the quantity. Sometimes the juice comes out too potent and you have to add water. Almost every house in Rwanda has a yellow plastic jug of banana beer tucked somewhere on the premises. It is like a mailbox in America or a teapot in England; everyone has to have one.

The beer is not really the important part; it is the friendship that it cements. Everywhere in my country you see people talking and laughing over bottles of banana beer. It most often happens at what we call *cabarets*, which are an indispensable part of life in rural Africa. They are like a bar and a convenience store combined, sometimes made of nothing but a few planks of wood. You see them on the sides of roads, in the suburbs, and even in the smallest little villages. Here you can buy canned goods, soap, soft drinks, batteries, toys, and all kinds of other things. The most important part of the *cabaret* is the front, where the owner has set out chairs, benches, and maybe even an old, ratty couch. This is where the local people, no matter what their station in life, will come together for a round of banana beer, often sipped through the same red straw. It is very hard to hate someone with whom you have shared a beer. There is too much laughter and good feeling between you. Even people who might be predisposed to be enemies will come together over a beer.

Perhaps this simple act taps into something in our national memory. Banana beer is known as "the drink of reconciliation." It plays an important role in our traditional local court system, known in the Kinyarwandan language as *gacaca*, or as it is loosely translated, "justice on the grass." If somebody had a problem with a neighbor he would not seek revenge. He instead brought it to the attention of a group of men who we called elders. They were not elected in the classical sense of ballots, but they were put in a position of leadership by a kind of unspoken common assent. To be an elder you had to have a reputation for fairness and sober judgment, something that would only become apparent over time. It was apparent in the way you lived your life. Hard-liners and loudmouths did not get to be elders.

The elders would invite the village to come sit under the shade of a tree and hear the opposing sides tell their stories. Almost all of the disputes concerned property. A stolen goat, for instance, or somebody trying to grow crops on a hill that belonged to another family. More serious cases—such as those involving violence—were always referred to the courts, but village elders were given wide latitude to help solve local problems.

After the two enemies had finished speaking, the elders would give their opinions, one by one, on what should be done to remedy the problem. It usually involved compensation. A typical punishment for a stolen goat would be to repay the man a goat—and then give him another as a fine. Somebody bringing a charge thought to be false would be ordered to pay the man he had slandered. Confession was always the key. The village put a high value on the act of admitting culpability, even if you were the one bringing the case. It was viewed as a necessary step in the process of absolution. A man who lied before the entire village knew that he would have to wear that lie for years to come. There was an enormous incentive to come clean, and very little penalty was meted out for being honest with the public, and with yourself.

Then came the most important part of justice on the grass: The two aggrieved men were required to share a gourd of banana beer as a sign of renewed friendship. There were usually no lasting scars because it was hard to stay angry at someone who had humbled himself before you. The adversarial system of justice practiced in the West often fails to satisfy us, I am convinced, because it does not offer warring parties the opportunity to be human with each other at the end. Whether you were the victim or the aggressor you had to strip yourself of pride and recognize the basic humanity of the fellow with whom you were now sharing a banana beer. There was public shame in this system, true, but also a display of mutual respect that closed the circle. Everyone who showed up to hear the case was invited to sip the banana beer too, as a symbol of the accused man's reconciliation with the entire people. It was like a secular communion. The lasting message for all that gathered there was that solutions could always be found inside—inside communities and inside people.

I am proud to say that my father was a respected voice in these sessions. He was usually the elder who spoke last, and his words therefore carried a great deal of weight. One case in particular stands out in my memory. The dispute was fairly typical—one man had planted a crop on a piece of ground that another family had claimed. A *gacaca* was called and the usual grievances were aired. Even a child like me could see that this was a case of a small misunderstanding that had blossomed into a full-scale war of pride. When two people dig in their heels against one another like that it takes quite a bit of mutual humbling for things to be put right again.

For whatever reason my usually imperturbable father was a bit out of patience that day. Perhaps the silliness of the case or the small-mindedness of the people concerned had finally gotten to him. When it came his turn to talk he stood up and motioned for the two warring neighbors to join him. They all walked out, with me trailing quietly behind, to the place on that particular hill where the disputed crop was planted. My father, in addition to being an elder, was also respected as a man who had a memory for land claims that went back generations. He saw at once that the crop had indeed spilled over onto the neighbor's land, but also that the majority of the field was where it should have been. There was no clear villain or victim.

"Listen, you two," he said, motioning with the blade of his hand. "*This* is where the line is. Respect it from now on, and respect each other as well. I don't want to hear about this again."

This was a vivid lesson for me.

My father spoke with the same kind of gravitas each January, on New Year's Day, when relatives from all over Rwanda were invited to a feast at our home on the hill. This is probably the most important day in the entire Rwandan calendar, even bigger than Christmas. Most people here identify themselves as Roman Catholic or Protestant, but we tend to emphasize New Year's Day as the time for extended families to come together and give each other presents and wish one another *bonne année*. It is also a holiday to reflect on the events of the past and one's hopes for the future, a fulcrum balanced on the tip of time. The meal served is always a belly buster. We would slaughter a bull for a feast of beef, and there were side dishes of beans and corn and peas and bananas, and, of course, banana beer.

After the meal was over my father would call me and my brothers and sisters to sit around him. He would give us all a verbal report card on our progress throughout the year of becoming good men and women. "You need to work harder in the fields," he would say to one. "You are doing well in school, but you must show more respect to your older brothers," he might say to another. As a good helper to my mother, and a quiet kid in general, my assessment was usually a kind one. Some parents might disagree with this discussion of a child's failures and accomplishments before the entire family, and I would agree that in the wrong hands it can be hurtful. But my father showed us the same compassion on these occasions as he showed in justice on the grass. His aim was never to embarrass us but to encourage us to do the right thing. Looking back on it I can say that I grew up knowing where the lines of good behavior were drawn.

My father had a favorite saying: "Whoever does not talk to his father never knows what his grandfather said." He was trying to express the linear quality of wisdom. His morality was not something that he made up on his own; it had been given to him by his own father and his grandfather before that, a mixture of Hutus and Tutsis stretching back hundreds of years to the time out of memory when our people had migrated to this hilly triangle between lakes. My father's sense of justice and kindness did not know ethnicity.

He often told us stories to make his thoughts clear, and one of my favorites was about the Rwandan concept of hospitality. We are a nation that loves to take people into our homes. I suppose our values are very much like the Bedouin of the Middle East, for whom sheltering and defending strangers is not just a nice thing to do but a spiritual imperative. Rwanda never had a hotel until the European colonists arrived. We never needed one, because a traveler between towns could count on having a network of people—friends of family, family of friends—with whom he could stay. We do this reflexively. Here is the story my father told me to illustrate the point:

> A party of hunters was chasing a wounded lion through the valley. The lion tried to take shelter in a man's house and the man decided to admit the lion, even though he was putting himself at great risk. The lion recovered from his wounds and was set free. And so if a man can keep a fierce lion under his roof, why can he not shelter a fellow human being?

Rwandans are expected to offer shelter to the distressed, no matter what the circumstances. I took this lesson as gospel, and I grew up believing that everybody felt this way.

TWO

WHEN I WAS FIVE YEARS OLD, there was an afternoon when people came to our house carrying spare clothes in their bags. My father seemed to know some of them, but not all. There must have been a dozen strangers in our courtyard. They were frightened and apologetic. "Don't worry, you're safe here," I heard my father say. "Relax and have a drink." There was one strange boy about my age. His shorts were filthy. There were cuts on his feet, as if he had been walking a long way. We looked at each other from across the courtyard.

I asked my mother what was happening, and she told me that there was trouble in the capital city. The white men who had been in control were having problems. Some bad things had happened, and these people who had come to visit us were trying to get away from bad men. They would be staying awhile.

We all slept outside that first night, and it was a bit of an adventure to be under the open sky. The adults smoked tobacco and talked in low voices.

On the second night I asked my father why we were sleeping outside and he told me the truth: "Because if somebody comes to burn the house down we will not cook to death inside it." The people who had come to stay with us were known as "Tutsis," he said, and there were people roaming about who hated them. It was hard for me to understand because they looked just like us.

I understood years later that our guests that November week had been fleeing widespread massacres in the wake of what was called the "Hutu Revolution of 1959." It was also when the tactic of burning down the enemy's houses was pioneered. Those who tried to protect the Tutsi were considered targets as well. To shelter the enemy was to become the enemy.

History is serious business in my country. You might say that it is a matter of life and death.

It is a rare person here, even the poorest grower of bananas, who cannot rattle off a string of significant dates in Rwanda's past and tell you exactly what they mean to him and his family. They are like beads on our national necklace: 1885, 1959, 1973, 1990, 1994. Even though this nation is dirt poor and our school system does not match the standards of the West, we might be the most knowledgeable people on the globe when it comes to analyzing our own history. We are obsessed with the past. And everyone here tries to make it fit his own ends. But this is not something of which we should always be proud.

George Orwell once said, "He who controls the past, controls the future," and nowhere is that more true than in Rwanda. I am fully convinced that when so many ordinary people were swinging machetes at their neighbors in that awful springtime of 1994 they were not striking out at those individual victims per se but at an historical phantom. They were trying not so much to take life as to actually take control of the past.

Rwanda is sometimes called the "Switzerland of Africa," and with good reason. Not only do people here tend to be quiet and reserved, like the Swiss, but our country is also a mountainous jewel tucked into some of the loveliest real estate on its continent. It is an aerie of high hills and grassy meadows and river valleys tucked between Lake Kivu to the west and the plains of Tanzania to the east. The entire region occupies an area no bigger than the American state of Vermont. It is so small there is usually never room for the name "Rwanda" on most maps of Africa and the word must be printed off to one side, sometimes with an arrow pointing to the pebble that is my country. But there is abundant rainfall and mild weather and black loamy soil that made it one of the richest spots in Central Africa for the growing of food and the herding of livestock. The good returns on small-scale agriculture therefore made it an attractive place to settle. And near the year 1500, at the same time that the arts and sciences were beginning to flower in Renaissance Europe, a distinct nation of people began to emerge in Rwanda under the banner of a dynastic king that everybody called the *mwami*.

According to tribal lore the bloodline of the *mwami* had a heavenly origin. If there was a dispute over succession the true king was supposed to be known by being born with the seeds of a squash plant clutched in his tiny fist. A court of royal advisers known as the *abiru* would reveal the successor when the current king died. They were also the guardians of the obscure poems, songs, and stories that comprised a kind of underground national history. It was a long account of violence and royal assassinations and illicit sex; in short, the failings of past kings and queens, the kind of history that doesn't flatter. It was known by a Kinyarwanda word, which is roughly translated as "gossip." If you were trusted with the gossip it was a signal that you were now a part of the inner circle. In Rwanda, political power has always been linked with control of history.

Kings were the ultimate guardians of the past and of power and they were supposed to watch over everybody with equal favor. They fielded extremely tough armies with excellent archers. As a result, we were one of the only regions in Africa where Arab and European slave traders were never able to conduct raids, and so almost none of our people were sold into bondage. One of our ancient kings—a ruler named Gihanga—was supposed to have discovered fire. A flame burned in his memory at the royal court until the monarchy finally ended in 1959. I'll say more about that event later, but it is important to know now that the early kings and all the advisers that surrounded them were generally the taller people in the tribe. This established a legend just as colorful as the squash seeds I mentioned, but one that would be infinitely more damaging.

It is well known that the main ethnic groups in modern Rwanda are the Hutu and the Tutsi, but it remains a matter of controversy if these are indeed two separate races or if that is just an artificial political distinction created in a relatively short period of time. Evidence points to the latter. We share a common language—the beautiful tongue of Kinyarwanda—the same religions, the same children's games, the same storytelling traditions, the same government, even, in most cases, the same outward appearance. We also had a strong idea of our hilly land as a unified nation and a pride in ourselves as tough warriors for the *mwami*. There was never any "Hutu homeland" or "Tutsi homeland."

What divided us was an invented history.

The false—but very common—explanation for our origins is that the Hutus are a wandering offshoot of the huge group of Bantu-speaking people who have occupied Central Africa for thousands of years. They were said to have come into the country from the west. The Tutsis, on the other hand, are supposed to be descendants of the taller peoples of the Ethiopian highlands near the headwaters of the Blue Nile. They were supposed to have invaded Rwanda from the north about five hundred years ago and established the *mwamis* government. Or so the story went. But there is no real evidence for it, and most scholars now think that it is pure invention. We will probably never know for certain. Africa's traditional history is one passed down through poems and genealogies and heroic ballads in which people, not places, are the emotional focus. So many specific details about geography and migration patterns are lost in the fog of time.

One influential man who helped create the "Tutsis from the Nile" theory was British explorer John Hanning Speke, who is given credit for being the first white man to lay eyes on Lake Victoria. He made some superficial observations about the people he came across during his expeditions in Central Africa and connected them with stories in the Bible. In his 1863 book, *Journal of the Discovery of the Source of the Nile,* he showed a strange fixation with an extended clan of leaders in what is now present-day Rwanda. These people—they called themselves Tutsis—measured their wealth in cows, drank milk, ate beef, and seemed to be taller and have slightly more angular noses than their subjects, who fed their families by growing cassavas, sweet potatoes, and other vegetables. Speke theorized that they were actually a lost tribe of Christians who had migrated from the deserts of the Middle East and were therefore the carriers of a noble line of blood. The Hutu—what Speke called the "curly-head, flab-nosed, pouch-mouthed negro"—was a different story. The name itself means "one who works," and Speke thought there was a divine purpose behind the differences in lifestyle.

Those who grew crops, he said, were probably the distant descendants of Noah's son Ham, who according to the ninth chapter of Genesis had committed the sin of looking at his father lying naked in a tent when he, Noah, was drunk on homemade wine. For this transgression Noah cursed his son Ham's descendants for all time. "The lowest of slaves will he be to his brothers," said the man who had captained the ark through the floodwaters. And, to Speke's way of thinking, these poor lowborns had obviously found their way to exile in Central Africa and had reproduced themselves by the millions. The Hutus were part of that accursed lot, and this explained their generally subservient role to the cattle-owning Tutsis, even though the two groups of people looked quite similar on the surface.

All of this is, of course, total European foolishness, but what came to be called the "Hamitic hypothesis" carried a surprising amount of weight in the late nineteenth century, just as the great powers were preparing to carve up Africa into colonies. These ideas about race were to become more than fanciful stories told over port at the Royal Geographic Society but an actual template for governing us. The real origin of Rwanda's class system had almost nothing to do with physical characteristics. It was much more banal than anything the European gentlemen explorers had been able to imagine.

What seems to have happened was that the ministers and priests closest to the Rwandan king started to conceive of themselves as being a special class of people, in much the same way that large landowners in what is now Great Britain or France began to call themselves lords and dukes and earls. In precolonial Rwanda, however, it wasn't land that was used to reckon a person's wealth. It was cows. Those who didn't have cattle were forced to turn to growing crops for sustenance and took on the identity of Hutu, or "followers". Many acquired cows by applying to a local strongman and agreeing to pay an annual tribute of grain and honey beer and pledging to defend him in times of war. These client relationships were known as the code of *ubuhake* and became the glue of the Rwandan social hierarchy.

Intermarriage between the Tutsi and the Hutu was not unheard of, but it was also not the norm. Those taller frames and aquiline noses that John Hanning Speke had fallen in love with were probably the result of just a few hundred years of sexual selection within that particular caste group. This deluded love affair, as you might guess, was soon to become the cause of great misery. I experienced it for the first time when I was nineteen years old.

My best friend, Gerard, was expelled from school in February 1973. This was one of the saddest days I had ever known, not just because I was losing my friend, but because it was my first real taste of the poison in the soil of my country. I also became aware for the first time of a bloodline inside me that divided me from people that I loved.

I had known Gerard almost as long as I could remember. We had both come from mixed families and we had a lot in common in the way we viewed the world. We had grown up together—played soccer together, talked about girls, made fun of each other, wondered together about our future careers, speculated about who we would marry—all the normal things that make up a friendship between boys. He was as smart a kid as I ever met. Our daily walk to school together had been a constant feature of my mornings ever since we were eight years old. Our footprints grew larger, but our friendship remained.

The year before Gerard was expelled there had been chaos and death in the neighboring country of Burundi, a nation with an ethnic composition very similar to Rwanda. The president, a former Army captain named Michel Micombero, had ordered his armed forces to crack down on a Hutu uprising, and these soldiers took their mission beyond the bounds of rationality. Nearly two hundred thousand people were slaughtered and even more fled their homes for the relative safety of my country. We have a saying: "Whatever happens in Burundi eventually spills over into Rwanda, and whatever happens in Rwanda will also spill into Burundi." And that was certainly the case in 1973.

The government in Rwanda was sympathetic and began taking reprisals against Tutsis as a kind of revenge. Several dozen were massacred with knives and machetes in villages near the border. Others lost their houses and their businesses.

The younger ones were kicked out of the schools. One of them was my friend Gerard.

I will never forget the last time we walked to school together. When we arrived there were lists of names tacked to the bulletin boards outside the classrooms. Gerard's name was there. He was told to take his things and go—he was not wanted at the school any longer. A group of Hutu students stood in front of the classroom door as a human wall to block the undesirables from going inside. These were the same children who had laughed, played, and gossiped together just twenty-four hours before. Now they were being divided in a way that was not fully comprehensible, but I will never forget the look of determination—even glee—on the part of some of my classmates who were accepting their new superior role all too readily.

I stood alone on the grassy quadrangle and watched Gerard walk back down the lane toward his home. That was the last I saw of him for a very long time.

His name was on the list because his mother was a Hutu and his father was a Tutsi. My name was *not* on the list because my mother was Tutsi and my father was a Hutu. Since ethnicity passes through the father's loins in Rwanda, according to this idiotic logic Gerard was considered a despicable Tutsi and I was considered a privileged Hutu. Had the parentage been reversed it would have been me walking down that lane of guava trees with my head down.

I cannot tell you how much I loathed myself that day for

having been lucky. It was the first time I became aware of myself not as "Paul" but as a "Hutu." I suppose this dark epiphany is an essential rite of passage for anyone who grew up in my country, one of the most physically lovely places on the globe, but one with poison sown in its heart.

I have to tell you more.

One of those beads I mentioned on our necklace is 1885. This was the year of the famous Conference of Berlin, which put the seal on what was to become nearly seven decades of colonial government in Africa. This was also where Rwanda's fate was to be determined.

Representatives from Austria-Hungary, Denmark, France, Great Britain, Spain, the United States, Portugal, Holland, Sweden, and Norway met to sort out the conflicting claims their agents had made to vast pieces of real estate in Africa—most particularly, the forests of the Congo that had been turned into a private reserve for King Leopold II of Belgium. The Berlin conference was remarkable not just for the lack of African participation, but also for laying out a few key principles. The first was that a European nation couldn't just draw lines on a map and claim that area as a protectorate. They had to prove they could "effectively occupy" and defend that territory. The second was that if a navy could seize a piece of coastline it would also have the rights to whatever lay inland for a virtually unlimited distance. The African continent was then sliced up with borders that frequently had no logical relation to watersheds, trade patterns, linguistic groups, or geography. Remarked the British prime minister: "We have been giving away mountains and rivers and lakes to each other, only hindered by the small impediment that we never knew exactly where they were."

Rwanda fared well in some ways—at least, better than most of our neighbors. The borders shaved some corners from the rugged area claimed by the *mwami,* but we retained a certain amount of territorial integrity. Our colonizing power would be Germany, a nation that generally did not share the worst rapacious tendencies of some of the other conquerors of Africa. They had won our aerie as a compromise and they showed little interest in taking advantage of what little natural resources we could offer them. It took German agents more than nine years to arrive in Rwanda and thirteen before they finally got around to establishing an administrative office. Our nation was assigned to the same colonial department as the neighboring nation of Burundi and renamed *Ruanda-Urundi.*

The Germans looked on their new possession with indifference. It was a country far from the ocean. The most important provision of the Berlin Conference—the one that required "effective occupation"—was also a problem. The government of Otto von Bismarck simply did not see the value in sending a large portion of its army and civil service to rule a poor chunk of landlocked farmland. What this meant, in effect, was that the kaiser's flag flew over our country as a matter of appearance, but the real power continued to be the top-down apparatus run by the Tutsi royalty. After the Germans' cata-strophic loss in World War I we were handed over as a spoil of war to the government of Belgium. That was the beginning of real change, for the Belgians showed more of an interest in us.

Belgium wanted to get the most profit out of Rwanda while expending the least amount of men and effort. The new colonizers looked at the social rift between our leaders and farmers and saw an easy way to rule by proxy. It was a version of the old divide-and-conquer tactics used so effec-tively by colonizers throughout history. The Aztec empire in Mexico was finished the moment that Hernán Cortés realized he could exploit minor resentments between tribes to his own advantage, making friends with one tribe to beat the more powerful rival and thus subdue the entire region for the Spanish Crown. And so the Belgians adopted the bizarre race theories of John Hanning Speke to turn the Tutsi aristocracy into something like junior managers. It was no longer enough to simply co-opt the royal court as the Germans had. There was now an explicitly racial way of separating the haves from the have-nots.

Here's how crazy it became. Belgian scientists were sent down to Rwanda with little measuring tapes. They determined that a typical Tutsi nose was at least two and a half millimeters longer than a Hutu nose. This brand of "scientific" race theory led directly to a particularly dark bead on our necklace: the year 1933, when all people in Rwanda received identity cards known as *books* that specified their ethnic class. Years later these cards would become virtual death warrants for thousands of people, as we will see. But the immediate effect of these cards was to crystallize the racism into a Jim Crow system. Almost all the colonial administrative jobs were reserved for Tutsis. When categories were written down, it became harder for Hutu to pass as Tutsi, even after they had accumulated many cows.

The doctrine of Tutsi superiority was taught in schools, preached in churches, and reinforced in thousands of invisible ways in daily Rwandan life. The Tutsi were told over and over that they were aristocratic and physically attractive, while the Hutu were told they were ugly and stupid and worthy only of working in the fields. An early colonial film described the farming class as "souls sad and passive, ignoring all thought for the morrow" who viewed their Tutsi masters as "demigods." This was the message that our fathers and mothers heard every day. One of the most distinguished scholars on our nation, the American professor Alison Des Forges, has described the net effect this way: "People of both groups learned to think of the Tutsi as the winners and the Hutu as the losers in every great contest in Rwandan history."

It saddens me to tell you that one of the archetypical images of my country became the Tutsi king borne on the shoulders of a platoon of Hutu laborers. It is true that my country, just as every civilization on earth, has economic and social inequalities in our past. What makes Rwanda particularly tragic, however, is that our unhappiness was given its shape by the indelible contours of race, making it all the easier for the great-grandsons of the whipped to find someone's head to chop off.

Rwanda's apartheid system began to fall apart in the 1950s, when it was becoming increasingly clear that the European powers could no longer hold on to their colonies in Africa. Independence movements were sweeping the continent—violently in some places, such as Kenya, Algeria, and the Belgian Congo. Nearly every nation that had participated in the Berlin Conference had been shell-shocked by World War II and no longer had a taste for empire. Under pressure from the United Nations and the world community, Belgium was getting ready to let go of its claim on Rwanda. But one last surprise was in store.

The Tutsi aristocracy had, not surprisingly, been generally supportive of their Belgian patrons through the years. But it was a devil's bargain. The Tutsis received a limited amount of power and a condescending recognition of the *mwami* in exchange for their ultimate loyalty to Brussels. They also co-operated in the oppression of the Hutu, who were forced to harvest timber and crops in crews of road gangs, with Tutsi bosses. As any social scientist can tell you, any system of organized hatred also damages the oppressor, if in less obvious ways. Tutsi were forced to punish their Hutu neighbors for misdeeds or face punishment themselves. And Belgium left no doubt who was in charge in 1931 when they deposed the *mwami* Musinga, who had resisted all the arguments of all the Catholic priests sent from Europe to convert the natives. The colonizers ignored the squash seeds and handpicked a successor, King Rudahigwa, a man considered sufficiently pliable. He was also an ardent Roman Catholic. His example led Tutsis and Hutus alike to convert to the new faith. Almost overnight Rwanda became one of the most Christian nations on the globe, albeit with a strong flavor of the old mysticism. The Catholic priests from Europe, however, helped foment a revolutionary twist in the history of Rwanda.

A well of sympathy for the Hutu underclass had been building throughout the late 1950s. The key role was played by the Roman Catholic Church. Perhaps it was the words of Jesus' Sermon on the Mount: "Blessed are the poor in spirit for theirs is the kingdom of heaven . . . blessed are the meek, for they will inherit the earth." Or perhaps it was that Belgium itself is a nation of competing ethnicities and that many of the Catholic priests sent to Rwanda were from the historically abused Flemish communities. Perhaps there was finally a sense that too much was too much. Either way, the authorities took steps to empower the people who had been suffering for so long. The

Hutus had always had superior numbers, and official policy began to reflect that mathematical reality—and then some. The Hutu slowly assumed power as the ruling class. One administrator in Kigali issued the following secret order: "I deem it necessary to rapidly put into place a local military force officially composed of 14 percent Tutsi and 86 percent Hutu but in effect and for practical purposes, 100 percent Hutu." Fearful of losing their longstanding grip on power—and perhaps also fearful of retributive violence—the Tutsi commenced a period of sharp opposition to Belgium's continuing hold on Rwanda. This course would prove disastrous for them, as it finalized the shift in Belgium's favor over to the Hutu they had mistreated for sixty years.

On July 27, 1959, our king died of a cerebral hemorrhage, and speculation ran wild that he had been secretly assassinated by the Belgians. His successor, the teenage ruler Kigeli V, would last only a few months before the ancient dynastic line would be snuffed out forever. Belgium called for the first free elections in Rwanda's history, but soon found itself trying to put down a rebellion of Hutu insurgents, who had set about murdering Tutsis and setting fire to their houses. Despite the centuries of coexistence, this marked the very first outbreak of systematic ethnic murders in Rwanda. The killers were rewarded with some of the first prosperity they had ever tasted. The homes, fields, and stores of the Tutsis often went into the hands of those who had hacked them apart, establishing a link between patriotism and money that has yet to disappear. I'll never forget sleeping outside at night during that time, wondering if somebody was going to burn our house down for harboring Tutsis.

The national elections were held in a climate of fear and—not surprisingly—the Hutus won 90 percent of the open seats. Suddenly it became desirable, even necessary, to have an identity card that called you a Hutu. Public schools were soon open to the majority, and children who had been denied education for years began learning to read and write and add figures just as adeptly as the Tutsi. This should have given the lie once and for all to Speke's idiotic racial ideas—as if they had not been discredited already. Belgium and the United Nations handed the nation over to a Hutu government and left the nation after a brief ceremony on July 1, 1962, at 10 o'clock in the morning. A new flag was hastily designed and raised: a tricolor banner with a plain letter R in the middle. These events, taken as a whole, came to be called the "Hutu Revolution." And there was to be no sharing of power.

Tens of thousands of persecuted Tutsis fled the country to the safety of Uganda and other neighboring nations. One of the refugees was a small child named Paul Kagame, who was said to have been carried on his mother's back.

Rwanda had not seen the last of him.

• • •

The exiled Tutsis would eventually number more than a quarter million. The angriest young men among them began launching guerrilla raids into Rwanda from their hiding places across the border. They were called "cockroaches" because they came out at night and were hard to kill. This military slang would soon be applied to the Tutsi people as a whole, a term as pernicious and dehumanizing as the American word *nigger*.

The raids were mostly amateur affairs, but they gave a pretext for our new government of President Grégoire Kayibanda to wrap itself in the flag of the Hutu Revolution and begin a purge of the Tutsis who remained inside Rwanda. There is no greater gift to an insecure leader that quite matches a vague "enemy" who can be used to whip up fear and hatred among the population. It is a cheap way to consolidate one's hold on power. And this is just what the new regime did.

The persecution was made all the eaiser because Rwanda is a meticulously organized country. The nation is arranged into a series of twelve prefectures, which look a bit like American states, except they have no powers. Within every prefecture are several communes, which are the real building blocks of authority in Rwanda. The head of the commune is known as the *bourgmeister,* or mayor, and he usually gets his job through a personal friendship with the president. This is the real seat of power in tiny Rwanda, which is like one giant village. Four out of five of us live in the rural areas and nine out of every ten people here draws some income from farming the hills. Even the most urbanized among us has a close connection with the backcountry. And so the orders came down to every hill: It was the duty of every good and patriotic Hutu to join "public safety committees" to periodically help "clear the brush." Everyone understood this to mean slaughtering Tutsi peasants whenever there was a raid from the exiles across the border. In 1963 thousands of Tutsis were chopped apart in the southern prefecture of Gikongoro. These countryside massacres continued off and on throughout the decade and flared up again after the trouble in Burundi in 1972 that caused the education of my best friend, Gerard, to be stolen.

He never quite recovered. Though he had the skills and the ambition to become an engineer, the only job he could get was selling banana beer in a stand by the side of the road. He later moved to Kigali, where he landed a clerical job in a bank. But he was always plagued by the image of what he might have become had he been allowed to continue his education and use all of the formidable talents that had rotted inside of him. When we were both much older I tried to get together with him for beers from time to time, but there was a taint of sadness, and even anger, that always hung over our friendship. I was one thing in the blood and he was another and there was nothing either of us could do to change it. He was a Tutsi by accident and he had to live the rest of his life under that taint, occasionally in fear for his life from the public safety committees and destined to work in dead-end jobs. It was an appalling waste—not just of a man but of a potential asset to Rwanda and the rest of the world. Gerard had something to give. It was not wanted.

As one born into the favored class, my accidental path would be different.

THREE

I SUPPOSE THAT every capital city in Africa—even those of
the poorest countries—must have a place like the Hotel Mille
Collines near its heart.

All the impoverished nations on earth, in fact, have these
few basic things: a flag, an army, borders, something resembling
a government, and at least one luxury hotel where the rich
foreign visitors and aid workers can stay. When operatives from
the Red Cross in Geneva or researchers from Amnesty International in London come here on their missions, they don't
stay in local guesthouses. They stay where they are treated to
high standards of comfort—even though they've come to work
on uncomfortable problems like AIDS, deforestation, torture,
and starvation. So there is always a demand for a spot of
opulence in a nation of mud houses. It is not all bad. A few
hundred locals get decent jobs as chambermaids, waiters, and
receptionists. Some elite suppliers get food and beverage
contracts. Most of the profits, however, are shuttled back to
whatever multinational company owns the property. The cost

for a room is usually equal to the yearly income of an average person in that country. I am not saying this is right. But this is the reality of modern Africa. And so in every impoverished nation on the continent, from Burkina Faso to the Central African Republic, you can inevitably find that one hotel a short walk away from the embassies where fresh laundry and gin and tonics are taken for granted and where there is an aura around the place that prevents any peasant from ever thinking of going inside.

In Rwanda, that place is the Hotel Mille Collines.

It is a modernist building of five stories, with a facade of stucco and smoked glass. From the outside it would look perfectly at home near any large American airport.

The Mille Collines was built in 1973 by the Sabena Corporation, which was the national airline of Belgium until it went bankrupt a few years ago. It was founded as the *Société Anonyme Belge d'Exploitation de la Navigation Aérienne,* a mouthful of a brand name later shortened to the acronym Sabena. It started off flying short cargo runs between Boma and Léopoldville and branched into passenger service. The executives foresaw the demand for an island of stateless luxury in the dirt streets of Kigali, and so they built the Hotel Mille Collines, aimed primarily at the diplomatic and humanitarian trade but with an eye toward snaring the occasional adventurous tourist on his way to see the gorillas in the north.

There is only one way in or out of the Hotel Mille Collines:

a two-lane driveway leading to and from the gate inside and the paved street outside. You could walk, it is true, but almost anyone who stays there would be driven in. The gate leads into a parking lot landscaped with colorful African plants and shrubs and surrounded from the outside world with a fence of bamboo poles. A line of flagpoles flies the national banners of Rwanda and Belgium and the corporate flag of the airline. There is a turnabout for cars to deposit their passengers at the lobby. You can feel the crisp blast of the air conditioner a few feet in front of the door. The lobby is tiled with sand-colored flagstones and decorated with potted plants and wicker couches. The staff behind the reception desk has been trained to greet all visitors cordially in French and English. There are a few shops that sell all the things a tourist might want: suntan lotion, aspirin, a carved figurine or a colorful African-print shirt as a gift. The indirect pinkish light filtering in through the big windows to the north and the tasteful fruit colors in the lobby give the place a tropical feeling. I have been told the entrance of the Mille Collines resembles that of beach vacation resorts in Fiji or Mexico. Off to one side is a small suite of offices for the general manager, the assistant general manager, and an agent of the airline.

Upstairs are 112 guest rooms, each one furnished according to the standards of upscale Western lodging. There are televisions with hundreds of satellite channels in multiple languages, beds with firm mattresses, shaving kits wrapped in protective plastic, circular cakes of soap. There are bedside phones guaranteed to give you a dial tone, a shower with safe water, a small strongbox with an electronic combination for your passport and money. The rooms smell like lavender cleaning solution. Those facing the pool are more expensive and have balconies shaped like half diamonds, where you can step out for a view of Kigali. Those facing the parking lot have false balconies so the sides don't look flat when viewed from the outside.

On the top floor is a small cocktail bar and also a set of conference rooms for visiting corporations or aid groups to hold their presentations. There used to be an unwritten rule in the elite circles that if your meeting wasn't held at the Mille Collines it wouldn't be taken seriously.

Down the hall from the bar and the conference rooms is the Panorama Restaurant. Here you can get escargots or chateaubriand or crab soup of a quality—and at prices—that match what you'd find in Brussels, Paris, or New York. Every morning there is an extensive breakfast buffet with good strong Rwandan coffee and five kinds of juices and a staff of waiters lurking discreetly in the background, watching for an empty cup or a dropped fork. If you're dining as a couple two servers will deliver the food to your table all at once so you will be disturbed for as brief a time as possible. The restaurant has no north wall—it opens up to a striking al fresco view of the Nyabugogo valley. You can see houses clinging to the far hillsides and the Boulevard of the Organization of African Unity, which runs to the north side of town and the airport. On the farthest hill in the distance is the black doughnut of the national soccer stadium, with banks of lights rising on poles from its outer walls.

The air in Kigali is sometimes hazy from farm dust and heavy with truck exhaust, but the view is always gorgeous and the sun never hits the dining tables directly. The Belgian architects saw to that by orienting the restaurant on a diagonal of the compass, away from both the sunrise and sunset. And when it rains, they simply close the blinds.

The most important place in the Hotel Mille Collines is on the lowest level. This is the rear courtyard, where there is a tidy lawn, a huge fig tree, and a small swimming pool without a diving board. There is also an open-air bar with about twenty tables and a few ceiling fans to push the air around. Ten more tables—the best ones—are set up in an L pattern around the pool.

Around this small square of water is where the real business of the Mille Collines is conducted. What takes place here far surpasses the day-to-day management worries of the hotel. Some people have even called it the shadow capital of Rwanda. You can probably guess why. It is *the* spot where the local power brokers come to share beer and ham sandwiches with aid donors, arms dealers, World Bank staffers, and various other foreigners who have some kind of stake in our country's future.

Worlds intersect here. Whites and blacks mingle comfortably here inside a thin cloud of cigarette smoke and laughter. Rick's American Café in *Casablanca* had nothing on the Mille Collines. I have seen cabinet ministers dispense appointments here, Army generals buying Russian rifles, ambassadors telling casual lies to presidential flunkies. The poolside is a place to advertise that you are a man with contacts and friendships. This is one of the best ways to climb the ladder in Kigali. These casual acquaintances are what can separate a wealthy man from a beggar.

I first laid eyes on the Mille Collines when I was nineteen years old. As a typical bored young man on my hill I hitched rides to Kigali whenever I could to wander the streets, browse through the markets, gawk at girls, and drink in the bars, all the typical idle pastimes of youth. The hotel had just been constructed and everybody was coming by for a look. It was then the tallest building in Rwanda and the first with an elevator. Few people had seen such a thing before. The big coup was to sneak inside and see if you could ride the elevator to the roof, where you could get a truly marvelous view of the valley below. Much to the envy of my friends back at home, I was able to charm my way past the bellboy and take that elevator ride up to the forbidden roof, where I savored a few stolen minutes of beauty. I remember feeling impressed with the hotel and proud of my country, thinking this place represented progress, and that a better way of life was on the way for all of us.

I had no idea just how large a role this strange new place was going to play in my life—or in the life of Rwanda.

I am a hotel manager by accident. The idea of having a career in the luxury hospitality business is certainly a laughable one for the son of a banana farmer from an impoverished African village. I never could have dreamed such a thing, nor could any of my friends.

I was supposed to have been a church pastor. This was a path that seemed preordained for me from a very young age. Everybody said I was suited for it because of my willingness to work hard, but even more because of my temperament. My peers in school—even those I wasn't close friends with—seemed to trust me with their secrets, and I always gave them advice that seemed practical to them. (You might say it was *igihango* all over again.) The teachers were also impressed with my ability to memorize sections of the Bible and rephrase them in plain language. They encouraged me to become a man of the church. It was always seen as the way up, at least to the people who ran my school. They belong to the Seventh-day Adventist Church, a very distinctive branch of Christianity. The Sabbath is celebrated on Saturdays, for instance, and Adventists make it a habit to avoid eating shellfish, pork, and other foods forbidden to the Jews. The most devout Adventists are vegetarians. They also do not believe in the idea of hell and live in intense anticipation of the second coming of Jesus.

On the top of a high hill overlooking the beautiful Ruvayaga Valley, missionaries had built a church and started a school for boys in 1921. They chose that piece of land because it had been used as an execution ground by a previous *mwami* and nobody from our area wanted to live there for fear of bad luck or death. The missionaries wanted to show their new followers that the old religions of Rwanda had no power and that their god was the only one. They eventually moved away to spread the gospel elsewhere, but their hilltop school remained. We called it a "college," but it was intended for students of all ages. It was designed in a simple but elegant manner, with the academic buildings arranged around a quadrangle. A row of teachers' houses lined the broad dirt avenue that led into town, surrounded with the now mature orange and guava trees planted by the pioneer churchmen. The centerpiece of the campus was a small stucco church in the European cathedral style, painted a soft blue. There was a large main classroom hall that looked like a railway station divided into four classrooms, each with tall windows and furnished with rows of severe wooden desks that had seats and footrests built into them. The plaster walls were painted the same baby blue as the church. Each room had a rectangle of black paint on the front wall that served as the blackboard.

I learned French at age eight, English at thirteen. I still remember the cover of the first book I ever owned, a textbook called *Je Commence,* or *I Begin.* I struggled the first year and resolved to do better. The next year my scores were among the highest in my grade and I saw my father's pride when my name was called during the honors assembly on the grassy quadrangle.

In religion classes they taught us Christian hymns. Some of them were tedious, but others were quite beautiful. My favorite was a mournful song called "The Salesman of Vaud" about a glamorous Swiss lady who wanted to buy some jewelry from a tattered old peddler, but all he had to give her was a copy of the Bible. She read it and her soul was saved. I had seen very few European ladies at the time, but those words seemed so sweet and wistful as we all sang them together inside the squat hilltop church:

> *Oh! Look at, my beautiful and noble lady,*
> *These gold chains, these invaluable jewels.*
> *You see these pearls of which the flame*
> *A flash of your eyes would erase?*

Though I seemed headed for a life of Christian modesty, there was always a streak of the entrepreneur in me. Even as a ten-year-old I was gathering up peanuts and reselling them for a profit. Hard work appealed to me. Where other teenage boys liked soccer and girls, my hobby was painting houses for people in the village. This was where I first learned the art of nego-tiation. I would start my price far above what I expected to receive and coyly ratchet it down according to what I saw in the face of the man who wanted his house painted. I earned a reputation as a tough bargainer but a conscientious painter. There was never any spot uncovered, and I used attractive shades of blue and indigo. I would get up very early in the morning to start a job, eat something small for lunch, and keep working through the fading light, until I could hear the gaso-line generators in town start up.

Though I earned good money I was never prey to bullies or to jealous thugs. I suppose I was adept at using the same skill at negotiation that made house painting such a lucrative business. If anybody tried to threaten me I would simply look him in the eye and ask him in a firm but friendly voice, "Why?" The bully would have no choice but to engage me verbally, and this made violence next to impossible. I learned that it is very difficult to fight someone with whom you are already talking.

On September 13, 1967, at the age of thirteen, I was baptized in the waters of the Rubayi River and was allowed to choose a new first name for myself. This is a ritual that merges a bit of traditional Rwandan culture with the Christian rite. To the endless confusion of outsiders, members of a single family here do not usually share the same last name.

My surname, Rusesabagina, was chosen especially for me by my father when I was born. In our language it means "warrior that disperses the enemies." I was allowed to choose a new first name on the day of my baptism and I chose "Paul," after the great communicator of the New Testament, the man who described himself in one of his letters as being "all things to all people."

While I seemed to have a natural gift for languages and banter, I was unfortunately not gifted in the art of making conversation with girls. They had a powerful fascination for me from the time I was about twelve or so, but I think I would have rather had a burning ember pressed into my tongue than talk to a pretty girl. So I never had a girlfriend in the conventional sense. But around the time that I was leaving my teenage years behind me and becoming a man, one young woman in particular started to develop an interest in me. Her name was Esther and she was the daughter of Reverend Sembeba, one of the African pastors of the Seventh-day Adventist Church and a very powerful man in the region. I fell in love with Esther and we made plans to get married. Our plan was for me to attend seminary and become a minister and she would come with me wherever I was posted. Then we would start having children.

My good behavior and my interest in religion earned me a scholarship to attend a school called the Faculty of Theology in the nation of Cameroon. It was more than a thousand miles from the hillside where I had grown up, but it would be a free education, and a good one at that. So on September 8, 1976, Esther and I were married in the baby blue church at the top of the hill. It was one of the happiest days of my life up until that point. I had presented her father with a cow, as is the Rwandan custom, and my friends brought in more cows to the reception as a symbol of the prosperity that the marriage was going to bring us. Milk from the cows was passed around and we held up the cups to one another. A few days later we said good-bye to everything that was familiar, caught a ride to Kigali, and boarded a flight to the city of Yaoundé. Neither of us had been on an airplane before.

I cannot say I have very fond memories of my time studying to be a pastor. Many of my fellow students were bright and eager, and I enjoyed picking apart biblical passages with them, but a good number of them also had no interest in being there. Quite a few of them were Tutsis who had no hope of finding any other job and were turning to the church for an escape from prejudice. The instructors taught us Greek so that we could read the New Testament in the original language. I cannot speak a word of this ancient tongue today, but I do remember the thrill of reading Christ's words. I still remember how powerful and in control I felt the first few times I delivered practice sermons before my instructors. But it became apparent to me that this was not a line of work I was suited for. For one thing, it seemed that the life of a pastor was going to be a dull one. I had tasted enough of the modernizing world to be enchanted with it—the airplanes, the elevators, the azure swimming pools—and the job of African gospel preaching did not go hand-in-hand with that kind of lifestyle. If I was going to lead a Seventh-day Adventist flock, I wanted it to be in Kigali at the very least, where I could live an urban life. But only a very few senior men, five at most, were privileged enough to have such a posting. And those men had won their prize jobs not through luck but through lifelong mastery of church politics. I looked into the future and did not like what I saw: a long sedentary life spent in a backwater village, getting older and hoping for a promotion that never came.

This anxiety about my future got me thinking about more troubling things. If I was not prepared to make such a sacrifice was I really cut out to be a worker in the Lord's vineyard? It was supposed to be the duty of every Christian to crucify his own flesh and put aside his own earthly desires for the sake of heaven. What did it say about my fitness for the pulpit if I was so disheartened about the road opening up in front of me?

It was in this unhappy state of mind that my wife and I moved to Kigali in December 1978. And it was there I found the place where I truly was meant to be. Or rather, it found me.

I had joined the great restless drift of young men who move to the capital city in search of something: a job, adventure, new girlfriends, the army, anything at all to break the dull monotony of country life. I think this is one of life's essential journeys and it happens in every nation and in every culture on earth: a young person in search of his fortune. During that wandering period before the age of twenty-five a man's shape is still undefined. His opinions tend to be passionate and wild but still essentially pliable, his character still open to molding by the friends or the circumstances that surround him. Several years after I arrived in Kigali the forces of history would do wretched things to the minds of those young men who had come in search of the same modest goals I was pursuing. But I am getting ahead of the story.

Kigali sprawls over more than a dozen steep hills near the geographical center of Rwanda. It is one of Africa's more relaxed capital cities, with a modern airport, a pleasantly unrushed market district, wide avenues shaded with jacaranda trees, and a notable lack of the desperate slum quarters that tarnish so many other African capitals. The main roads are well paved and free of potholes. Most of the architecture is of the late-1960s institutional style and the majority of houses are made of the same adobe bricks and corrugated metal roofs you see in the backcountry. But on clear evenings you can climb to the top of Mount Kigali and look out over the chain of valleys and the soft twinkling lights on the hillsides and think that the old proverb is true, that God wanders the world during the daytime, but comes home to Rwanda at night.

An irony of my country is that the capital is in this beautiful place because of the racial divide. There wasn't much of anything here except a small town next to a dirt airstrip until 1961.

That was when the new government realized they could no longer stomach the idea of keeping the capital in the old royal Tutsi city of Nyanza, where the *mwami* had held court. The tiny village of Kigali, in the center of the country, was chosen as a new seat of government, mostly because it was a place that had no precolonial history, and therefore no baggage. In that sense it is a city very much like Washington in the United States or Canberra in Australia—an artificial capital plunked down in an obscure place to help quiet factional jealousies. When Esther and I moved into a rented house with our two young children in 1978 I resolved that I would stay here no matter what happened. I had found my place.

Fate had intervened, as it so often does, in the form of a friendship. I had a playmate from childhood named Isaac Mulihano who worked behind the front desk at the Mille Collines. He had heard through the gossip mill that I had dropped out of the seminary and so he sent a message to me back on the hill where I was staying for a few weeks. "Come work with me in the hotel," he said. "We have an opening and you would be perfect."

The hotel already occupied an exalted spot in my mind—it was the symbol of urbanity I had been craving—and I seized the chance to be a part of it. So I put on a white shirt and a tie and learned the art of how to put people in the right rooms, how to arrange for fresh flowers and taxi rides, and how to handle complaints with a smile and quick action. I seemed to excel at this last skill. It is one of the most complicated parts of working in a hotel—and where a service reputation can be made or broken. If you show the guest you really care about his problem and make him feel as though he is getting his way (even when he isn't) it will give him a positive feeling about the hotel and the staff and make him inclined to come back for a repeat visit. I learned that most people just want to feel as though they are being heard and understood. It is a simple lesson, but one that so many seem to forget. The other clerks began to let me handle the really sticky complaints. I learned that I could usually make even the most irate guests leave the front desk at least a little mollified if I showed them I was listening.

Month followed month. I worked hard at my job. My managers were impressed with my command of French and English as well as with the cheerful attitude I tried to bring to work every day. At that time, a Swiss company named Tourist Consult had a contract to train all the new employees, and they put me through the program. While I was trying to make sure I was doing everything right, the training director, Gerard Rossier, came up to me and asked, "Why are you working at the front desk?"

The question surprised me.

"This is the job that I enjoy," I told him.

"You are not in the right place," he told me, and explained that Tourist Consult was offering ten free scholarships to the hospitality program at a college in Nairobi. I knew English and French and seemed like a responsible enough young man.

Would I be interested in applying for one?

I thought that over for about half a second before saying yes.

The application process was only a formality. The only thing I needed was a signature from a government minister, who had to personally approve all the scholarship recipients. And this was where I got my first real taste of the patronage system.

The rift in my country is not just between Hutus and Tutsis. There is also a rivalry between Hutus from the northern part of the country and Hutus from everywhere else. After President Juvenal Habyarimana came to power in 1973, a tight circle of his friends from the north part of the country, especially people with family ties in towns like Gisenyi and Ruhengeri, managed to dominate all the key cabinet posts and high-paying civil service jobs. The minister, of course, hailed from the north, and I fell into that category of Hutu that came from everywhere else. I was also a desk clerk, the son of a banana farmer. Nobody with any political connections, either. That made me nobody, period. He refused to sign my application. Of course, they would not say so directly.

"Has he gotten a chance to sign my application?" I asked the secretaries.

"He is still reviewing your application. You should have an answer soon."

I went back every day for a week and got the same answer. All the other scholarship recipients received their signatures, but mine was in an endless state of review. It became clear that more was holding up my application than just the usual molasses of bureaucracy. Even though my career was on the line, I would not allow myself to get angry. I understood immediately that it was all about business. It was not as if the minister had anything against me personally. It was that the hotel scholarship was now a commodity—no different from a case of beer or a Honda motorcycle. If I took that last slot it would be one less favor he could do for a hometown relative or a political acquaintance. Giving his signature to me would have been giving it for free, because I had nothing to offer.

It was a dismal lesson in politics. But I will never forget the counterlesson I learned from Rossier when I told him I couldn't go to the college after all.

"Oh, really?" he said. "Why not?"

"The minister will not sign my application."

"I see," said Rossier. "Let me take care of things."

My signature came that very afternoon. I found out later that a simple message had been conveyed: Either Paul gets your signature today or we will never offer hotel scholarships to anyone in Rwanda again.

It seemed that there were multiple ways to solve a problem. And I was a fast learner.

In Nairobi I learned many more things. I learned about the various wine-growing regions in France, and how to tell Bordeaux from Burgundy. I learned what separates a good Scotch from an excellent one. They sent me to Switzerland, where I learned even more about fine wine and food. I learned how to do book-keeping, write a budget, manage a payroll, hire and fire, plan institutional goals. And I learned the art of performing courtesies without making a show of it. The idea is to not be noticed in the act of doing something nice for somebody, but, of course, people will notice. People *always* notice.

I grew in confidence as a manager, but my personal life was not so happy when I was at college. Time and distance took a toll on my marriage. Esther and I grew further apart, and we separated in 1981. I was granted legal custody of our three children, our daughters Diane and Lys, and our son Roger. It was a wrenching experience, one of the saddest periods in my life, but I was sure of at least one thing when I came back home to Rwanda. My career path was at last known to me. I would be a hotel man, not a preacher. The Hotel Mille Collines was something like an old friend to me by then. My troubles in marriage had made me bitter and hurt, but I threw myself back into my work with vigor and not a little bit of relief. It became my solace.

I have since come to realize that those years studying to be a churchman were not wasted at all. It was where I acquired knowledge that helped to shape my future. I gained an even greater understanding of human beings—what motivates them, where their failings are, where the good might be found that can trump the evil inside. Another thing the ministry teaches you is how to present a forceful case in language that everyone can understand. Learning to be a preacher makes you a better talker. That was one skill that would certainly come in handy in my personal life. I discovered, for example, that I had lost my shyness around girls.

One day in 1987 I was invited to a wedding. I have never been a good dancer and so I sat on the edge of the crowd, nursing a beer and watching people dance. I could not take my eyes off a particular woman in a white dress. She was the maid of honor. She had a shy smile that made my stomach turn over like an upended bowl of pudding. I cannot remember to this day what we talked about, but I remember thinking that her ideas were as fresh as her appearance. We exchanged phone numbers and said good-bye, but I did not forget her. I learned that Tatiana worked as a nurse in the town of Ruhengeri in the north. She happened to be a Tutsi. I could not have cared less about that, but other people certainly did. She was suffering a huge amount of prejudice at her workplace and she wanted to leave.

At last, a matter of the heart where I knew what to do! I went straight to work. The minister of health was a frequent guest at the poolside of the Mille Collines and I arranged a favor. Tatiana soon received a transfer to Central Hospital in Kigali. By that time my divorce was final and I was a free man. I courted my new girlfriend assiduously and we married after two years. Diane, Lys, and Roger accepted Tatiana as their new stepmother almost immediately. Tatiana conceived and gave birth to a daughter, who perished before she could be given a name on the eighth day, according to the Rwandan custom. It made us all grieve. But before long, my wife was pregnant again and we brought my son Tresor into the world. And I settled into a loving family life, feeling like a complete husband and father once more.

My stock continued to rise at the Mille Collines, where I was made an assistant general manager. They gave me an office of my own, as well as the authority to dispense little perks here and there to favored guests. An Army general who came in frequently would get a free cognac, or perhaps a lobster dinner. It made them feel appreciated, which is a universal hunger among all human beings. The gifts were also an indication of their status in front of whatever companion they had brought in. This helped to not only cement their fidelity to the hotel, but to make them appreciative to me personally. If we had an important diplomatic visitor, I would give them the royal welcome at the front roundabout, asking them in courtly European tones about their trip and telling them we had a very nice room waiting for them, even when it was occasionally not so nice.

I learned to take my morning coffee not in my office but down at the poolside bar. At 10:00 A.M. some of the capital's big shots would start to drift in. Some of them came in alone with reams of paperwork. Others brought their friends and coworkers. Most had the thick Rwandan coffee, some breakfasted on beer. The talk was a stew of personal chitchat and government business. I don't know why so many of them thought of the Mille Collines as an office out of the office. Perhaps the walls had ears at their ministries. Perhaps it just felt more relaxed here. Whatever the case, an astonishing number of decisions were made next to the pool, and I watched it all happen from my perch at the bar. I learned to tell from subtle body language whether I should approach a table for some welcoming banter or whether it was best to remain invisible.

I know that my promotion was resented among some of the people I had worked with at the front desk. Some of them started to call me a certain name behind my back: *muzungu*, the Kinyarwandan word for "white man." We used to yell it out gleefully to European aid workers and missionaries when we were kids. It was not insulting in that context. But applied to me it was meant to be insulting; the equivalent, I am told, of the American phrase "Uncle Tom." I suppose this should have gotten under my skin, but it did not. For one thing, jealousies and backbiting are common to any place of work. Show me a place where more than ten people are employed, and I'll show you a coiled spring where everybody's favorite game is called *who's up, who's down* (I confess to having played it myself). For another thing, I never felt as though I was being untrue to myself. Just the opposite: I was learning a great deal about the way my country really worked and meeting people who had grown up in circumstances even poorer than mine. We had gotten where we were due to hard work and determination. Never once did I feel as though I was being untrue to the life my father had wanted for me since the first day he took me to school at Gitwe and told me that if I was willing to do the work I would be successful in the world.

I do not agree with those who say that you cannot be successful and authentic at the same time. If advancing in the world is viewed as a form of treason, then we are all in trouble.

So I tried not to let the mutterings of *muzungu* bother me, but a day came when I had to assert myself to my old friends at the front desk. The flashpoint was a phone call. Somebody had telephoned the Mille Collines and asked to speak with "the African general manager." The call was clearly for me, but the receptionist, an old colleague of mine, insisted on taking the call himself. I think he wanted to show that he didn't think much of me anymore. After that incident, I took him aside.

"Listen, my friend," I said. "Today, I am your boss and you must respect me."

I made the same kind of point to my white coworkers, and again it was over something trivial. All the top department heads were supposed to meet weekly to discuss various issues, and these sessions required a secretary to take notes. I was always asked to do this. Eventually, I asked that the duty be rotated with each meeting, and my colleagues quickly agreed.

A small point, but one that earned me respect in the long run.

Year followed year. I kept climbing. In 1992, I was made the general manager of the Hotel Diplomates, the other capital city luxury hotel owned by Sabena. It was a smaller property barely a half mile up the hill from the Mille Collines, but no less prestigious. The Diplomates catered mainly to ambassadors, presidents, prime ministers, and other dignitaries visiting Rwanda from other parts of Africa and the world. There were sixteen big luxury suites, forty regular rooms, a wide lawn, a resplendent terrace, and a very good restaurant called The Rotunda. I was no longer working in my beloved Mille Collines, but this was a huge step up the ladder. I had become the first black general manager in the company's history.

It was a small distinction, I suppose, but I only wish my father could have seen it. He had died the year before, at the age of ninety-three in a hospital in the town of Kibuye, where he had gone for surgery. The light was still in his eyes the last time I saw him. He said a curious thing. "Listen, my son. You might meet hyenas on their way to hunt. Be careful." It was very typical of him to talk in these kinds of parables, but I have wondered many times about what he meant. Perhaps he was just telling me to be careful that day on the drive back to Kigali. Perhaps it was meant to be a caution for the years to come. I'll never know because my father died later that day. He was so important to me, a man who taught me most of what I know about patience, tolerance, and bravery. He had always wanted me to come back to my home to be the mayor, and I suppose on this count, I hadn't quite lived up to his expectations. But I still knew that he had been terribly proud of the work I was doing in Kigali and that he loved me. I could not ask for too much more than that.

I regret immensely not being able to do something important for my parents before they left the world. They had given me their best when I was a child and, now that I was a grown man, I wanted to build them a new house on the hill or do something else to make sure they were comfortable. This is the Rwandan way. But shortly before my father died, my mother had gone in for a routine doctor's visit and they found a cancer inside her. This strong and lively woman quickly grew frail and I was powerless to do anything about it. The last words she ever said to me were spoken from her hospital bed. "Son, I am going to my house now," she told me. I can only hope that, wherever she is today, her house is more splendid than anything I could have ever imagined for her.

As the general manager of the Diplomates I had to do a lot of negotiating. There were food contracts to be signed, employee grievances to be addressed, conference rooms to be booked, wedding receptions to accommodate. More often than not I conducted these talks inside the bar or in the restaurant. I had learned how friendship and business can be artfully juxtaposed without corrupting each other.

Let me explain. We have a saying in Rwanda, a leftover from the brief time when we were a colony of the Germans: "*Dienst ist dienst, und schnapps ist schnapps.*" It means "work is work and booze is booze." There were often sticky issues to work through in my new job, but I had long ago discovered the value of a compartmentalized mind. You could never let your opinion of a person interfere with the business between you. He may be your best friend or somebody you detest, but the conversation should not change. *Dienst ist dienst.*

I met many people in Rwanda whose racial ideology I couldn't stand, but I was unfailingly polite to them, and they learned to respect me even though our disagreements were obvious. This led to a priceless realization for me. Someone who *deals* can never be an absolute hard-liner. The very act of negotiation makes it difficult, if not impossible, to dehumanize the person across the table from you. Because in negotiation you will never get 100 percent of what you want. You are forced to make a compromise, and by doing this you are forced to understand, and even sympathize with, the other person's position. And if cups of good African coffee, some wine, a cognac, or all of the above could help lubricate this understanding, it was all to the good.

So I spent as little time as possible shut up inside the walls of my office. I took my morning coffee at the bar, watched the comings and goings, made careful note of who the regulars were, followed the gossip about their careers, and saved up that knowledge for the frequent times when I would find myself clinking glasses of complimentary Merlot with a man whose friendship was another link to the power web of the capital and whose favor I could count on in the future. And the presence of beverages always kept the tone easy and social, even when the subtext of the discussion was quite serious.

It was just like my father had said: "You never invite a man without a beer."

FOUR

ON AUGUST 8, 1993, a new radio station went on the air. It called itself Radio-Télévision Libre des Mille Collines. I would come to wish that the name of this station wasn't so similar to that of my beloved hotel.

The station broadcast at 106 on the FM dial and called itself by the call letters RTLM, in the American style. It billed itself as the very first private radio station in the country, and it was an immediate sensation. It started by playing Congolese music virtually nonstop. I am not a man who particularly likes to dance, but even I can tell you that this is a fun, bouncy, energetic type of music to which you cannot help but move your feet a little. RTLM then started to broadcast a few human voices, like a shy child finding its courage. The disk jockeys began to talk more. Then they started telling mildly dirty jokes. Then they started a call-in format in which ordinary Rwandans could hear their own voices broadcast over the air. People began calling in with road information, song dedications, complaints about local politicians, rumors, speculations, opinions, chatter. We have a saying here about the nature of neighborhood gossip. We call it *radio trottoir*—or, the "radio of the sidewalk." RTLM was the radio of the sidewalk suddenly blasted out to the whole country.

I can't begin to tell you how revolutionary this was. Unlike the dull government marginalia you usually heard on the official Radio Rwanda, RTLM was fresh. It was irreverent. It was *fun*. It constantly surprised you. It was giving us what we wanted but in a way that was lively and modern and American. Even those who were offended were hooked. It was the giddiness that comes with looking at your friend in shock and saying, Can he really *say* that? Yes, I think he just did.

Just as Rwandans are serious about history, we are also serious about news. You see small battery-powered radios everywhere in our country. They are playing on the edges of cornfields, inside taxicabs, in restaurants and Internet cafés, balanced on the shoulders of young men and old women and on the kitchen tables inside mud-and-pole houses on distant hills. Official announcements here can be as dry as sawdust, but we always pay attention. Perhaps it taps something in our national memory of the godlike pronouncements from the royal court of the *mwami*. It always amazes me how people in Europe and the United States can be so indifferent to the speeches of their chancellor or president, for these words from the top can be a wind sock for what might happen next.

RTLM pulled off another feat. It convinced ordinary

citizens that it could be trusted to give a truthful account of what was really going on inside the nation. And it did this by taking a skeptical attitude toward the current president, Juvenal Habyarimana. For a people who had been raised on a diet of official propaganda, this was something new indeed. Any voice that was less than worshipful toward the president *had* to be independent. There was even an aura of crusading journalism about the station, which did not hesitate to publicize the names of the bureaucrats who were supposed to be responsible for paving a potholed road or prosecuting a market thief.

As the winter faded into the new year of 1994, the talk on the radio grew bolder and louder. Listeners couldn't help but notice that almost every broadcast seemed to feature an overarching narrative. And that story was that the country was in danger from an internal threat and the only solution was to fight that threat with any means necessary. There were daily on-air debates that represented two sides—the extremist and the even more extremist. The station had helped gain credibility by shaming lazy government officials. Now it started to name ordinary citizens. And the tone began to change. A typical broadcast:

> Jeanne is a sixth-form teacher at Muramba in Muyaga commune. Jeanne is not doing good things in this school. Indeed, it has been noted that she's the cause of the bad atmosphere in the classes she teaches. She

urges her students to hate the Hutus. These children spend the entire day at that, and it corrupts their minds. We hereby warn this woman named Jeanne, and indeed, the people of Muyaga, who are well known for their courage, should warn her. She is a security threat for the commune.

I wanted to stop listening to RTLM, but I couldn't. It was like one of those movies where you watch a car speeding in slow motion toward a child in the middle of the road. It doesn't seem real. You wince, you even want to scream, but you cannot look away.

In fact, when I think back on what we all heard on RTLM in those strange slow-motion months before April 1994 it seems impossible that we could not have known what was coming.

It always bothers me when I hear Rwanda's genocide described as the product of "ancient tribal hatreds." I think this is an easy way for Westerners to dismiss the whole thing as a regrettable but pointless bloodbath that happens to primitive brown people. And not just that, but that the killing was random and chaotic and fueled only by brute anger. Nothing could be further from the truth.

There is a reason why Rwanda's genocide was the quickest one in recorded history. It may have been accomplished with crude agricultural tools instead of gas chambers, but eight hundred thousand people were killed in one hundred days with a calculated efficiency that would have impressed the most rigorous accountant.

Those "tribal hatreds" were merely a cheap way to motivate the citizen killers—not the root cause. It is phenomenally dangerous to dismiss Rwanda in this way, because it steals one of the most vital lessons all this bloodshed has to teach us.

Make no mistake: There was a method to the madness. And it was about power. What scared our leaders most was the idea that Rwanda might be invaded and their power taken away. And in the early part of the 1990s that threat was very real.

The Tutsis who had fled the mobs years earlier for the safety of neighboring countries had always dreamed of returning home. Under the leadership of General Fred Rwigema, and subsequently of Paul Kagame (the same child who had fled the country on his mother's back in 1959) they organized themselves into a military force called the Rwandan Patriotic Front. These soldiers were far outnumbered by the Rwandan army, but they still constituted an impressively disciplined and effective band of fighters. On October 1, 1990, they crossed the border and started moving toward the capital. This was not the amateurish vandalism of thirty years earlier. This was a real invasion.

Three nights later, when the RPF was still a long way from Kigali, there was a clatter of gunfire all around the capital, including some mortar shelling. The next morning the government made a stunning announcement: Some rebels had managed to infiltrate their way into the heart of the nation and had staged a sneak attack. Only the bravery and talent of the Rwandan Army had saved the country from disaster, and only the deceit and cunning of traitors within the neighborhoods had made the attack possible.

It was all a charade. What really happened is that some trusted Army soldiers were dispatched to various neighborhoods and told to fire their weapons in the air and in the dirt. The effect of the "surprise attack," as you might guess, was to spread fear that an enemy was hiding among the population. It was a cheap but effective way for President Juvenal Habyarimana to rally the people to his side and shore up his weakening hold on power. Thousands of innocent people, mostly Tutsis and those perceived to be their sympathizers, were rounded up and thrown in jail on trumped-up charges. The minister of justice proclaimed that the attack could not have happened without the collaboration of hidden *ibyitso,* or "accomplices," and a curfew went into effect on the streets of the capital.

I have said that a false view of history is a toxin in the bloodstream of my country. With the start of the civil war the myth-making machine went into high gear. There was suddenly no distinction between Tutsis and exiled RPF rebels; they were lumped into the same category of rhetoric. The war itself was cast as an explicitly racial conflict. And ordinary

Rwandans started to arrange their lives around this idea.

My troubles with the president began when I refused to wear his picture on my suit jacket.

I suppose it was my private act of rebellion against President Juvenal Habyarimana, who I considered a criminal and a blowhard. He was a bit on the fat side, and walked with a slight limp that was said to be an old Army injury. He sparkled in his suits, which were all tailored in Paris. I was especially irritated by his habit of clearing out the national parks of tourists so he and his cronies could go on big game hunting trips. In my position it would have been incredibly unwise to give voice to these thoughts, so I kept them to myself. But I drew the line at those stupid portrait pins.

Like many African "big men," Habyarimana had a penchant for plastering his face on billboards and public spaces everywhere throughout the nation. I suppose it is a combination of vanity, insecurity, and old-fashioned advertising strategy that makes leaders do this. If enough people get used to associating his name with pomp and power over the years they'll become reluctant to want to ever throw him out of office. Suffice it to say, Habyarimana loved his own face so much that he eventually decided that his subjects should carry it on their breasts. He designed medallions with his own photograph in the middle. These were sold to various people—commune administrators, priests, wealthy businessmen—with instructions to wear them while acting in their official capacities. The Roman Catholic archbishop of Kigali helped set the tone by wearing the portrait pin on his cassock while saying mass.

On the twenty-fifth anniversary of Rwanda's independence, a big state dinner was held at the Hotel Mille Collines. All the national big shots were there, as well as foreign dignitaries, including the king and prime minister of Belgium. I wore my best white suit for the occasion. But, of course, I had no portrait pin in my lapel.

One of the president's thugs came over to me just before the ceremony was to begin.

"You are not wearing your portrait of the president," he told me.

I agreed with him that this was the case.

He grabbed me by the collar, yanked me out of the receiving line, and told me that I would not be greeting the president that night. It took the well-timed intervention of my boss, the chairman of Sabena Hotels, to make things right. Either I would be restored to my place in the receiving line or the hotel would refuse right then to be the host of the Independence Day dinner. It was probably a bluff, but it worked. I went back into the line and shook the president's hand without his face grinning up from my lapel.

The very next morning another of his goons showed up at the front desk of the Mille Collines and asked for me. When I didn't appear he handed the headwaiter a brown envelope and told him to deliver it to me. It was stuffed full of Habyarimana medals.

"From now on," he told the headwaiter, "your manager will wear one of these every time he comes to work. We will be watching. The rest of these medals are to be given to the employees."

The next morning I showed up to work without wearing a medal. A black car arrived at the front door roundabout and I was escorted over. They told me I now had earned "an appointment" at the office of the president. I followed them there in a hotel car and allowed myself to be led into a side office, where I was screamed at for several hours.

"You do not respect the boss, our father!" they screamed at me.

"What did I do wrong?" I asked, although I knew.

"You stupid man, you did not wear your medals! Why not?"

"I don't see the benefit in doing that," I said.

It went around and around like this before they kicked me out of the office—with a literal foot planted on my butt—and a command to be back the next morning. And the next day, they screamed at me for hours and gave me another kick in the butt before they let me go.

It went on like this every day for a month. I was no longer working at the hotel, just reporting to the office of the president. His thugs became my daily escorts. We started to get used to each other and exchanged morning pleasantries before the daily screaming began. And I would always tell them the same thing: "I really don't see why I should wear the medal."

The irony of this show of muscle was that the president was not really in control of his own power base. Everybody who was well informed in Rwanda knew that he was essentially a hollow man, largely the pawn of his own advisers. He had risen up through the defense ministry and was put in charge of the purge against the Tutsis in 1973 that had been responsible for the deaths of dozens and wasted the futures of thousands more, including my friend Gerard. In the midst of all the chaos, Habyarimana launched a coup and took over the presidency of Rwanda, promising to bring an end to the violence. His real talent was squeezing money out of international aid organizations and Western governments while at the same time shutting down any internal opposition. He formed a political party called, without apparent irony, the National Revolutionary Movement for Development and conferred mandatory membership on the entire country. Every person in Rwanda was supposed to spend their Saturdays doing work for the government: highway repair, digging ditches, and other tasks. If it ever occurred to him that this was basically a repeat of the forced labor policies of the Belgians and the *mwami* he never showed much concern about it.

The people who benefited most were Habyarimana's friends from the northwest part of the country. We called these people the *akazu*, or "little house." Their main channel of access to the riches of government was actually not through the president but his strong-willed wife, Madame Agathe. If you weren't from the northwest, or weren't close with Madame, you stood little chance of advancing. I had discovered this unfortunate reality of life in 1979, when Tourist Consult had to use that strong-arm tactic so that I, a man from the south, could get a college scholarship. Having friends in the *akazu* became even more important after the world price of coffee plunged in 1989 and the Rwandan economy collapsed with it.

Empty suit that he was, Habyarimana had managed to stay in power through the depression with the help of the government of France, and particularly because of the French president, François Mitterrand. These two presidents got along famously and shared many dinners. Mitterrand even gave our president his own jet airplane. Loads of development money and military assistance flowed to us from Paris throughout the years. When the RPF launched its attack in 1990 and the Rwandan Army exploded in size from five thousand soldiers to thirty thousand to counter the threat, France was there to help train the new recruits. In some cases white French soldiers came quite close to actually fighting the rebels, with some instructors aiming artillery cannons at RPF positions and stepping back to let Rwandan soldiers press the fire button. As much as twenty tons of armaments a day were airlifted into Kigali courtesy of Habyarimana's friends in Paris.

The French love affair with Rwanda was, you might say, also

a product of a pervasive national mythology. "France is not France without greatness," Charles de Gaulle had said, and the preservation of that status as a global leader defines much of the policy thinking in the offices of France's Foreign Ministry on the Quai D'Orsay in Paris. Maintaining a strong web of economic and diplomatic interests in their former African colonies is seen as a key part of that strategy. And so in places like the Ivory Coast, the Central African Republic, and Chad, where the French tricolor flew until the 1960s, France has provided monetary support, trade links, and frequent military intervention almost from the day that these countries gained their independence. Its eagerness to play such a father-figure role earned it the nickname "the policeman of Africa." The French army, in fact, has executed nearly two dozen military campaigns on the continent since the era of independence—a level of microinvolvement far out of proportion to any other great power. France never was much of a player in Rwanda during colonial times, but they now considered us worthy of attention for their own psychologically complicated reasons.

If Rwandans are obsessed with height, then the French are obsessed with tongues. A large part of that mystical *greatness* in the French mentality is centered on the preservation of the pure French language and the repelling of all attempts to marginalize it in favor of the international tongue of commerce, aviation, and diplomacy that is English. President Habyarimana and the Hutu elite were considered exemplary guardians of the French language and the kind of cultural values that it represented. At the urging of his French friends, our presidential "father" instituted new educational guidelines in schools, and new ways of teaching mathematics and the French language to young people.

The RPF invaders, by contrast, had spent most of their lives exiled in the former British colony of Uganda and were therefore English speakers, part of what amounted to a representation of the old Anglo-Saxon hordes that had been dogging France for the last thousand years. And I believe they were not entirely wrong—I believe the English speakers did have their own ambitions to achieve hegemony in the region and control the entire space between the Indian Ocean and the Atlantic. So at the Quai D'Orsay the logic went like this: If the RPF rebels should become strong enough to overthrow Habyarimana it will spell the loss of a small but important Francophone ally in Central Africa, which could soon be speaking English as an official language, reviving unpleasant tribal memories of the Battle of Agincourt and the Hundred Years War. While the French publicly supported peace talks, they were, in reality, working behind the scenes to preserve Habyarimana's shaky hold on power.

I am not saying this mentality is logical, but if there is anything that being a Rwandan has taught me, it is that most politics is an outgrowth of emotions that may or may not have any relation to the rational.

So when I decided not to wear the president's portrait on my lapel I was putting my thumb in the eye of a very insecure man. My friends told me later that I had been taking a stupid chance. I should have just worn the stupid thing to make the flunkies happy and not risked my job or my family's welfare on a symbolic matter. I knew Habyarimana and the *akazu* didn't much care for me, anyway. It would have cost me a huge amount of self-respect to have worn that dictator's face on my jacket. If this was a risk, it was a calculated one.

I never told my father about my run-in with the president. I didn't want him to worry about my job—or my life. But if I had told him, I like to think it would have made him laugh.

• • •

While peace talks with the rebels dragged on the programs on RTLM got worse and worse. I do not know how I managed to keep listening to it. Perhaps it was out of a need to understand exactly where popular opinion was heading. Or perhaps it was just morbid fascination.

Either way, I began to hear the racial slur "cockroach" so frequently that it lost whatever power it had to shock. I heard myself being lumped in with those who were considered less than human. The enormously popular singer Simon Bikindi had recorded a song played over and over on RTLM called "I Hate These Hutus." He was talking about people like me— those people of the majority group who didn't have a taste for

racial politics and refused to join in the crude political movement that became known as Hutu Power. To Bikindi they were
nothing but traitors:

> I hate these Hutu, these arrogant Hutus, braggarts who scorn
>   other Hutus, dear comrades.
> I hate these Hutu, these de-Hutuized Hutus, who have dis-
>   owned their identities, dear comrades.

The anger on the airwaves became so common that it didn't
seem particularly out of line when RTLM broadcast the tape of
an address made at a political rally in the northwest town of
Gisenyi. The speaker was a government official named Leon
Mugesera and, I have to say, he knew how to whip up a crowd.
Copies of this speech had already been circulating around the
country like bootleg treasures, with people commenting
favorably that here was a man who really understood the threat
to Rwanda. "Do not let yourselves be invaded," he kept exhort-
ing the crowd, and it gradually became clear he was making
an allusion to the ruling party being "invaded" by moderates
who wanted to engage in peace negotiations with the pre-
dominately Tutsi rebels. In words that would become widely repeated throughout Rwanda, he also recounts a story of saying
to a Tutsi, "I am telling you that your home is in Ethiopia, that
we are going to send you back there quickly, by the Nyabarongo."
Nobody in Rwanda could have missed what he was really

saying: The Tutsis were going to be slaughtered and their bodies thrown into the north-flowing watercourse.

His final exhortation to the crowd could have served as a summary of the simpleminded philosophy of those who were screaming for Hutu Power the loudest: "Know that the person whose throat you do not cut will be the one who cuts yours." He was preaching an ideology—and an identity—based on nothing more than a belief in the murderous intentions of the enemy.

I think that was the most seductive part of the movement. There is something living deep within us all that welcomes, even relishes, the role of victimhood for ourselves. There is no cause in the world more righteously embraced than our own when we feel someone has wronged us. Perhaps it is a psychological leftover from early childhood, when we felt the primeval terror of the world around us and yearned for the intervention of a mother/protector to keep us safe. Perhaps it makes it easier to explain away our personal failures when the work of an enemy can be blamed. Perhaps we just get tired of long explanations and like the cleanliness of an easy solution. It is for wiser people than me to say. Whatever its allure, this primitive ideology of Hutu Power swept through Rwanda in 1993 and early 1994 with the speed of flame through dry grass.

The grand purpose, as I have said, was not really to avenge the slights committed by the Tutsi royal court sixty years earlier. That was merely the cover story, the cheap trick that could rouse a mob into supporting the strong men. And *that* was the true purpose of all the revolutionary rhetoric: It was all about Habyarimana and the rest of the elite trying to keep a grip on the reins of government. It seemed almost irrelevant to point out that Hutus had been in a position of undisturbed power for thirty-five years and that the Tutsi were in a position to affect very little of Rwanda's current miserable situation—even if they had wanted to. It was a revolution, all right, but there was nobody to overthrow.

The Hutu government wanted all the anger in Rwanda pointed toward any target but itself. RTLM was officially a private venture with an independent editorial voice, but the extent to which it was an arm of the government was kept a secret from most Rwandans. Few people knew, for example, that the station's largest shareholder was actually President Habyarimana himself. The other financiers had close ties to the *akazu*. They included hundreds of people, including two cabinet ministers and two bank presidents. The station was officially in competition with the government station, but was allowed to broadcast on their FM 101 frequency in the mornings. Like most radio stations, RTLM had an emergency power source in case of blackouts, but this one was not a generator on the back lot. It was apparently an electrical line that led straight into the house across the street, which happened to be the official residence of none other than President Habyarimana.

I have mentioned those talk radio "debates" on RTLM that were really just shouting matches between two people who only disagreed about the best way to make the Tutsis suffer. You might wonder how any audience could stand to listen to such obvious garbage. How could the Tutsis—and those who loved them—not have made a protest or at least fled the country when they heard such irrational anger growing stronger and stronger? Could they have not read the signs and understood that hateful words would soon turn into knives?

Two factors must be taken into account. The first is the great respect we Rwandans have for formal education. If a man here has an advanced degree he is automatically treated as an authority on his subject. RTLM understood this and hired many professors and other "experts" to help spread the hate. The head and cofounder, in fact, was a former Ph.D. professor of—what else?—history.

The other thing you have to understand was that the message crept into our national consciousness very slowly. It did not happen all at once. We did not wake up one morning to hear it pouring out of the radio at full strength. It started with a sneering comment, the casual use of the term "cockroach," the almost humorous suggestion that Tutsis should be airmailed back to Ethiopia. Stripping the humanity from an entire group takes time. It is an attitude that requires cultivation, a series of small steps, daily tending. I suppose it is like the famous example of the frog who will immediately leap out of a pot of boiling water if you toss him into it, but put it in cold water and turn up the heat gradually, and he will die in boiling water without being aware of what happened.

RTLM was not the only media outlet turning up the heat while the rebel army inched across the countryside. Mugesera's throat-cutting speech was played on Radio Rwanda. And in 1990 a new newspaper called *Kangura* (*Wake It Up*) started publishing. It was essentially RTLM in print—populist, funny, and completely obsessed with "the Tutsi question." Its publisher was Hassan Ngeze, a former soft-drink vendor from Gisenyi who most people considered a loudmouth and a boor. He bragged about fictional deeds in his past, exaggerated the circulation numbers of *Kangura,* and obtained many of his scoops from his connections in government ministries. But he had an amazing talent for crystallizing people's dark thoughts and splashing them on the pages in an entertaining way. And just as RTLM was bankrolled by wealthy people close to the president, this rag was secretly funded by members of the *akazu.*

By August 1993, the rebel army had scored several convincing military victories in the north and put Habayrimana in a position where he was forced by France, the United States and other Western countries into signing a peace treaty known as the Arusha Accords. He surely must have recognized it as his political obituary. It laid the foundations for a power-sharing government. Habyarimana would be allowed to stay on as president, but only in a ceremonial sense. And in a special insult to all those who hated the Tutsi, a battalion of six hundred RPF soldiers was allowed to occupy the grounds of the parliament building in preparation for the formation of the transitional government. *Kangura* portrayed these troops as the point of a spear aimed straight at the heart of the Hutu majority. The paper also made a curious prediction: President Habyarimana would not live out the year. He would be assassinated, said the paper, by a rebel hit squad. It would then be the duty of every good and patriotic Hutu to seek revenge. Otherwise, the rebel army would start killing innocents.

In a February 1994 article headlined "Final Attack," Ngeze wrote: "We know where the cockroaches are. If they look for us, they had better watch out." Other features were not as subtle. "What weapons shall we use to conquer the cockroaches once and for all?" queried the caption of one illustration. The answer was pictured to the side: a wood-handled machete. Children were clearly enemies, too. "A cockroach cannot give birth to a butterfly," proclaimed one story. Another diatribe went like this: "We say to the cockroaches that if they lift up their heads again, it will no longer be necessary to fight them in the bush. We will start by eliminating the *internal* enemy [my italics]. They will be silenced."

This farce of a paper had a small circulation but an enormous reach. Copies were sent out to the villages and passed around gleefully. It seemed a welcome break from the usual tired and boring news out of the capital. Here at last, said many people, is a paper that really says the ugly truth—that the Tutsis are going to kill us when they invade.

Before it stopped publishing two months before the genocide *Kangura* editorialized: "We must remark to the cockroaches that if they do not change their attitude and if they persevere in their arrogance, the majority people will establish a force composed of young Hutu. This force will be charged with breaking the resistance of the Tutsi children."

What the newspaper did not say was that just such a force had already been put into place and was busily preparing itself to murder children throughout Rwanda.

In early November 1993, a shipment of cargo was trucked into Kigali. The wooden crates bore import papers announcing that they had been received from China at the seaport at Mombasa in Kenya. Inside were 987 cartons of inexpensive machetes. This was not enough to cause alarm by itself. The machete is a common household tool in Rwanda, used for all manner of jobs—slicing mangoes, mowing grass, harvesting bananas, cutting paths through heavy brush, butchering animals.

If anybody had been paying attention, however, the shipment might have seemed curious when matched with other facts. The recipient, for example, was one of the primary financial backers of the hate-mongering radio station RTLM.

Those cartons from China, too, were but a small part of what amounted to a mysterious wave. Between January 1993 and March 1994, a total of half a million machetes were imported into my country from various overseas suppliers. This was a number wildly out of line with ordinary demands. Somebody obviously wanted a lot of sharp objects in the hands of ordinary Rwandans. But nobody questioned the sudden abundance of machetes—at least not publicly.

If those imports were quiet, the formation of the youth militias was obvious. It was hard to miss those roving bands of young men wearing colorful neckerchiefs, blowing whistles, singing patriotic songs, and screaming insults against the Tutsis, their sympathizers and members of the opposition. They conducted military drills with fake guns carved from wood because the government could not afford to give them real rifles. They were known as the *Interahamwe,* which means either "those who stand together" or "those who attack together," depending on who is doing the translating.

Habyarimana's government formed them into "self-defense militias" that operated as a parallel to the regular Rwandan army and were used to threaten the president's politicial enemies. They were also a tool for building popular support for the ruling regime under the all-embracing cloak of Hutu Power. The ongoing civil war brought a whole new flock of members. Most of the new recruits came from the squalid refugee camps that formed a ring around Kigali. It is difficult for me to describe just how terrible the conditions were inside these camps: no decent food, no sanitation, no jobs, no hope. There were several hundred thousand people crammed into these tumbledown wastelands, most of them chased away from their homes in the countryside by the advancing RPF army. Kigali itself held about 350,000 people at the time—a city about the size of Minneapolis, Minnesota—and the strain on the infrastructure was very great. These refugees saw plenty of reasons to be angry at the rebels—and, by unfair extension, angry at each individual Tutsi. Plus, the militias were *fun,* in the same way that the hate radio was fun. They brought a sense of purpose and cohesion to an otherwise dreary life. It was like being in the Boy Scouts or a soccer club, only there was a popular enemy to hate and a lot of built-up frustration to vent. The boys were also hungry and full of the restlessness of youth. It was easy to get them to follow any orders imaginable.

The groundwork for the genocide went even deeper. In the fall of 1992 mayors in each of Rwanda's hundred little communes were asked by the president's political party to compile lists of people—understood to be Tutsis and people who were threatening to Habyarimana—who had left the country recently or who had children who had left. The implication was that these people had joined the ranks of the RPF. These lists could then be used to identify "security threats" in times of emergency. Tutsis throughout the country suspected their names were being entered into secret ledgers. Many tried without success to have their identity cards relabeled so that they would appear to be Hutu.

I used to be in the habit of stopping off at a bar near my home after work and buying a round for some of my friends from the old Gitwe days. One afternoon when I wasn't there, a man wearing the uniform of a soldier tossed a grenade in the door and sped off on a motorcycle. The bar was destroyed. I started going straight home after that. The minister of public works, Félicien Gatabazi, was gunned down by thugs as he was entering his house. A taxi driver witnessed the assassination; she was shot as a precaution the next day. Her name was Emerita and she had been one of the freelance drivers who competed for fares in the parking lot of the Hotel Mille Collines. At least one hundred other innocent people would be killed in this fashion by the increasingly violent teenagers of the *Interahamwe* and also rebel soldiers who had infiltrated Kigali. People didn't want to stand at bus stops or taxi stations anymore because the crowds were targets for grenade throwers.

A scary incident happened on the road. My wife, Tatiana, was driving our son to school when she was forced off the road by a man in a military jeep. He walked over to her door, took off his sunglasses, and bid her to roll down her window.

"Do you know me?" he asked.

"No," said my wife.

"My name is Étincelles," he said. It was the French word for "explosions," apparently his nom de guerre.

He went on: "Madam, we know your home. We know you have three big German shepherds in the yard for protection, as well as two gate guards. The Youth of the Democratic Republic Movement has said they plan to kidnap you. They will be trying to get ransom money from your husband. So I am telling you, if anybody should try to pull you over, don't stop. Keep driving, even if you have to run somebody over. Do it for your own safety. I am telling you all of this because I come from the same part of the country as your husband and I don't want to see any harm come to you."

When my wife told me about this I searched my memory for anyone from my village who might be calling himself Étincelles. I couldn't think of who it might be. To this day I have no idea if this was an actual kidnap plot or just an attempt to scare us. Regardless, we no longer felt comfortable living at home after that, and so I moved us all into a guest suite at the Diplomates. It felt awful to be governed by fear, but these were very dangerous times. I did not want anybody coming through my windows.

Life went on, even in the surreal twilight of that spring. At nights on the terrace I would share beers with the leaders of the militia movement, trying to keep quiet as I heard them talking of events in the neighboring country of Burundi. The president there, Melchior Ndadaye, had been assassinated by Tutsi officers in his own army. A series of reprisal killings followed. The international community had little to say about these massacres. Was it true the Tutsi were planning to do a similar thing here: take power and then start a campaign of genocide against the Hutu? I heard it said more than a few times over glasses of Carlsberg or Tuborg: "It may come down to kill or be killed."

During that dangerous time I did something that had the potential to be my death warrant. The RPF leadership was looking for a place to give a press conference and every public venue in town had rejected them. When they approached me about a room at the Diplomates, I agreed to host them, and I charged them the standard rate of five hundred dollars. It wasn't the profits I cared about. I really believed they deserved to have equal access like anybody else. It was not my place to discriminate based on ideology or what people would think of me. But I heard later that the government was unhappy with me. I suppose, in retrospect, it was like the incident with Habyarimana's silly medals. These were symbolic stands, and probably foolish, but ones I thought were worth the risk.

I have said that those first months of 1994 were like watching a speeding car in slow motion heading toward a child. There was a thickness in the air. You could buy Chinese-made grenades on the street for three dollars each and machetes for just one dollar and nobody thought to ask why. Many of my friends purchased guns for themselves in the name of home protection. This was something I refused to do, despite the urging of my wife. In one tense conversation she told me I was acting like a coward for not acquiring a firearm. "You know that I have always said I fight with words, not with guns," I told her. "If you want to call me a coward for this, then I guess that is what I am." She stared back at me, hurt and silent.

A few days later, I took her and our little son, Tresor, along with me to a manager's meeting in Brussels that I had been scheduled to attend. With the other children at boarding school in Rwanda, it was just the three of us, and we made a little vacation out of it. We traveled by train through Luxembourg, Switzerland, and France. Walking amid the gray monuments and plazas, drinking the yeasty beer, and eating the starchy tourist food made it possible—almost—to forget the slow boil back at home.

After three weeks, I had to return to my job, and we arrived in Kigali on the red-eye on the morning of March 31. At that hour the city was quiet, the militias were mostly asleep and the tension that I had come to associate with Rwanda was at low ebb. The rolling green hills had never looked so good or so welcoming. Perhaps things were finally calming down. The United Nations had sent twenty-seven hundred troops to Rwanda a few months earlier to enforce the Arusha peace agreement, and it seemed the visible presence of the blue helmets was finally making a difference in keeping the militias contained. The UN seemed capable of maintaining the peace. They had given us hope.

It had been so long since we had been to our house that we decided to go straight there instead of to our suite at the Diplomates. For the first time in almost two years we felt good about the future.

FIVE

I STILL REMEMBER the sunset on that night of April 6, 1994. There was no rain. The sky was hazy with spring moisture and dust and the slanted dying light made the bottoms of the clouds turn blood orange. The colors deepened and darkened as the sun went lower, reaching for the hillcrest in a nimbus of purples, violets, and indigos, the colors of oncoming night. Around town some people paused to watch, cocking their heads to the west. It was a moment of beautiful stillness.

I have been told that it is common for people to mark exactly where they are when they learn of death on a grand scale. I have met Americans, for example, who can tell me in detail which suit they were putting on or what highway they were driving down at the time of the suicide jet attacks on the World Trade Center. Perhaps it is a way to link our own small presence to the great bloodstained currents of history for just a moment. I suppose this is also a way of feeling a part of an overwhelming fa-

tal event, a slight flirtation with the finality that awaits us all—
a rehearsal for our own deaths, you might say.

I know with certainty that you will find nobody living in
Rwanda today who does not remember what they were doing
in the early evening hours of April 6, 1994, when the private jet
of President Juvenal Habyarimana was shot down with a
portable missile as it approached for landing at Kigali Airport.

As it happened, I was in my usual place for that time of day.
I was eating a dinner of panfried fish on the terrace of the
Diplomates Hotel. Sitting next to me was my brother-in-law.
We were celebrating a small victory—I had helped his wife get
a job as a saleswoman for a Dutch car dealer named NAHV.

The airport is about ten miles away and so we heard nothing
out of the ordinary. Less than a minute after the crash, however,
the waiter came over with a house telephone. It was my wife on
the line.

"I have heard something I have never heard before," she told
me. "Get home as fast as you are able."

I couldn't have known it then, but phones were ringing all
over the city and would continue to ring all night long.

On the way out to the parking lot we talked to an Army
major who had been listening to his radio. Roadblocks were
going up all over town, he told us, though he could not explain
why. Don't take the Gikondo road, he said. Take the one that
leads past the Parliament. Oddly, this was where the rebel army
had its local stronghold. My brother-in-law shook hands in the

parking lot and we urged each other to be careful. I could not have known it then, but I was shaking his hand for the last time.

I drove on the Boulevard of the Organization of African Unity through Kigali, which was unnaturally deserted. The power had been cut off and all the street lamps were off. There was virtually nobody on the streets. I saw glimpses of cooking fires flickering behind adobe walls, an occasional face mooning out from the shadows. It occurred to me that a coup d'état might be taking place, or perhaps the long-awaited RPF invasion. But I was calm. For some reason it did not occur to me to be frightened.

I drove slowly and carefully, but passed no other drivers. Kigali was like a city battening down before the arrival of a hurricane. It was 8:35 P.M.

The killing could have ended right there. It all could have been stopped quite easily at this early stage with just a small fraction of the police department of any midsized American city. Rwandans have always shown respect to authority figures—it is part of our national personality—and a brigade of international soldiers would have found it surprisingly easy to keep order on the streets of Kigali if they had had the guts to show they meant business about saving lives. But they didn't.

A force of twenty-seven hundred United Nations peacekeeping soldiers was already inside the country. But they were ill equipped and under strict orders from UN headquarters not to fire their weapons except in defense of themselves. "Do not fire unless fired upon" was the mantra. The recent U.S. disaster in Somalia, in which eighteen Army Rangers had been killed by street mobs, had made the idea of "African peacekeeping" a poisonous concept in the minds of many diplomats in the American State Department and the UN Security Council. They saw nothing to gain from it and everything to lose.

The leader of the UN troops in Rwanda was a lantern-jawed general from Canada named Romeo Dallaire. None of us knew it at the time, but he was handcuffed by a lack of resolve from his bosses in New York. He and his troops also had no idea what they had gotten into. In terms of background intelligence, Dallaire had only a map of Rwanda ripped out of a tourist guide and an encyclopedia entry hastily photocopied from the Montreal Public Library. But he got a quick and nasty education about Rwanda after an informant from a high level of the Hutu Power movement sneaked over to the UN compound one night, that winter. This man, later nicknamed "Jean-Pierre," came with a story that would have seemed incredible to anyone who hadn't been watching the frog slowly boiling for the last year. Up to seventeen hundred *Interahamwe* members had apparently been trained to act as an extermination squad against civilians. There were secret caches of arms scattered all around Kigali—stores of Kalashnikovs, ammunition, and many more of those damnably cheap grenades—to supplement the militia's arsenal, which consisted largely of traditional Rwandan weapons like spears and clubs. Jean-Pierre himself had been ordered to register all Tutsis and opposition elements living in a certain area, and he strongly suspected it was being prepared as a death list. Those who were planning the genocide expected there to be some half-hearted resistance from the UN at the beginning, said Jean-Pierre. And there was a strategy to cope with this—a brutal attack aimed at Belgian soldiers serving with the UN mission. It was thought that the Europeans would have no stomach for taking casualties and quickly withdraw their troops, leaving Rwandans to shape their own destiny.

In disregard of his UN superior in Rwanda, Jacques-Roger Booh-Booh, Dallaire had not sat on this news. On January 11, 1994, he had sent a cable to his superiors in New York informing them of his intention to raid the arms caches. It would have put only the tiniest dent in the amount of sharp-edged killing weapons being stockpiled around Rwanda, but I believe that it would have inflicted a devastating psychological blow to the architects of the genocide. They would have seen that somebody was paying attention and that genocidal actions would be met with reprisals. But the response Dallaire received from his UN bosses nicely summarized just about every cowardly, bureaucratic, and incompetent step this organization was to make in a nation on the brink of mass murder. Stockpiling of weapons may have violated the peace accords, Dallaire was told, but going after them was "beyond the mandate" of the United

Nations. He was instead encouraged to take his concerns to a man who surely would be the last one in the world to care: President Habyarimana.

The UN official who directed General Dallaire to take this deferential action was the chief of peacekeeping, Kofi Annan, who would one day serve as secretary-general.

Jean-Pierre's warnings were effectively brushed off. Nobody from the UN ever heard from him again.

So it did not stop.

The guards opened the gate for me at my house, and I walked through my front door to the sound of a ringing telephone. It was Bik Cornelis, the general manager of the Hotel Mille Collines—my counterpart at Sabena's other luxury hotel. He was a colleague and a friend, and not one to waste time when something was pressing.

"Paul," he said, "your president and the president of Burundi have been murdered."

"What?"

"Their plane was shot down with a rocket just a few minutes ago and they are both dead."

My wife and I stared at one another from across the living room while I tried to digest the meaning of these words. The only clear thought I could manage was that Tatiana must have heard the sounds of a plane exploding. I had no idea what that must have sounded like.

"All right," I said to Bik. "What does this mean?"

"I don't know," he said. "We don't know what is going to happen. But I think you'd better go back to the Diplomates. We don't know what will follow this."

"All right," I said. "But I don't think I should go alone. I'm going to call for a UN escort."

"Whatever you think is best," he said. "I will be in touch."

We hung up and I told my wife the news while I dug in my pants pocket for a phone number. Tatiana looked as if she might faint. There was no need for us to discuss the gravity of the situation. We both knew Rwanda's history. Murders at the top are usually followed by slaughters of everyday people. And since I was such a political moderate and she was a Tutsi we were both in trouble. How much time would we have before there was a knock at the door?

I picked up the phone.

The leaders of the UN troops had always been cordial to me on their frequent visits to the hotel, and they often said things like, "If there's anything you need, please call the compound and we'll see what we can do for you." This seemed like a good time to play that card. I was put on the line with the commander of the Bangladeshi troops that made up the largest contingent of the United Nations' mission in Rwanda. I had heard rumors about their poor training and lack of equipment, but they were wearing the uniform of the UN, which carried a kind of magical protection for them. Unlike nearly everybody else, they could pass roadblocks without harassment by the militia.

"I need a military escort to the Diplomates Hotel," I told him. "Can you help me?"

His voice sounded very far away, as if he was speaking from down a long hallway.

"People have already started killing other people," the major told me. "They are stopping people at roadblocks and asking them for identification. Tutsis and those in the opposition are being killed with knives. It is very dangerous to go outside. I don't think I can help you."

"Well, what am I supposed to do if they come here looking for me?" I asked.

"Does your house have two doors?"

"Pardon me?"

"Does your house have more than one way to get inside?"

"Yes, of course. There is a front door and a backdoor. Why?"

"It is very simple. If the killers come looking for you through the front door, just leave through the backdoor."

I thanked him for this advice and hung up.

It seemed that this was going to be all the help we would get from the United Nations tonight. I resigned myself to staying at home that night and hoping that nobody would come through either door.

My next phone call was to my friend John Bosco Karangwa, who was someone I could always count on for a good laugh. I knew he would be at home alone—his wife was in Europe for medical treatment. John and I had been in the moderate political party together—the Democratic Republican Movement, or MDR—and we shared a mutual dislike for Habyarimana. John hated him with a special passion. To tease John Bosco I sometimes referred to the president as his "uncle." Even though I knew Habyarimana was a criminal, he had been ruling Rwanda for more than twenty years, and it seemed surreal that he was gone.

"Your uncle has been killed," I told John Bosco.

"What?" he said. "Are you sure?"

"Yes. They shot down his plane about an hour ago."

"Let me confirm this before I start celebrating," he said.

We shared a little laugh, and then I got serious with him. I hated thinking about my friends according to their ethnicities or loyalties, but now was no time for reflection. A crude equation was now in effect. John Bosco was in the political opposition party and the assassination could spell only very bad things for him.

"Bosco, you could be killed tonight," I told him. "I want you to stay inside, keep your lights off, and let nobody inside your door."

I am happy to tell you that I received John several days later as a refugee inside my hotel. He had been in hiding in his house as he had promised. A friend had delivered his younger brother's three children into his care because the brother and his wife had been murdered. When I finally saw John Bosco, he hadn't spoken above a whisper for days. We made no more jokes about the death of the president.

Pieces of the story started filtering in from the radio that night. President Habyarimana had been flying back from Tanzania, where he had been negotiating how to implement some provisions of the Arusha peace agreement. On the plane with him was the new president of Burundi, Cyprien Ntaryamira; the chief of staff of the Rwandan Army, Déogratias Nsabimana; and nine other staff members and crew. At approximately 8:30 in the evening, as the plane was approaching the airport, two shoulder-launched missiles were fired from near a grove of banana trees in the Masaka neighborhood. One of them struck the fuselage of the president's Mystere-Falcon 50 jet, which had been a treasured gift from French president François Mitterrand. The fuel tank exploded and the fragments of the plane rained down over the Masaka commune. Some of it landed on the lawn of the presidential palace. There were no survivors.

It remains a mystery to this day who fired these missiles. One credible theory is that the rebel army had learned of the president's flight plan and decided to take down the plane as a military tactic. We may never know for sure. But whoever did it must have known that the immediate effect on Rwanda would be catastrophic.

With the death of its president the nation of Rwanda was officially decapitated. Members of the *akazu* gathered around a conference table at Army headquarters and allowed Colonel Théoneste Bagosora—the father of the *Interahamwe*—to effectively take charge of the country. Romeo Dallaire was at this meeting and he urged the new crisis committee to allow the moderate prime minister, Agathe Uwilingiyimana, to take power, as she should have. They refused, calling her a traitor. But she was a problem they would not have to suffer for long.

Later that night Agathe called the UN detachment and asked for more security. She wanted to go to Radio Rwanda in the morning to tell the nation not to panic, that a civilian government was still in charge. How little she understood. Rwandan Army soldiers were already surrounding her home in the dark shadows of the jacaranda trees. When fifteen UN soldiers arrived in the hour just before dawn they were welcomed with a burst of gunfire that shredded the tires and wrecked the engines of two of their jeeps. The prime minister, frightened and screaming, climbed over her back wall into the house of a neighbor.

I was listening to the buildup of this disaster being broadcast live on Radio France International. It was preposterous and macabre and pitiful and terrifying. Agathe's hiding place in the toilet was discovered and she was led outside in the midst of a cheering mob. There was a brief argument among the Rwandan soldiers over whether she should be taken prisoner or executed on the spot. The squabble ended when a police officer, who had been training to be a judical officer, stepped forward and shot the prime minister in the head at close range. The bullet tore away the left side of her face and she bled to death right there on the terrace in front of her house.

The UN soldiers, meanwhile, were persuaded to give up their weapons and led to Army headquarters near the heart of downtown, right across the street from the Hotel Diplomates, as it happened. Five of the soldiers were from Ghana and they were allowed to go free. Ten of them had the misfortune of being from Belgium—the colonial master country, the ones who had glorified the Tutsis and made them like kings. RTLM had been passing the sentence for the last few hours: The Belgians were already "suspected" of being the ones who had shot down the president's plane. This was in conflict with the line that was already becoming like gospel on *radio trottoir*—that it was the RPF rebels who had sneaked into Kigali with a shoulder missile and hidden in the weeds near the airport, waiting for the wink of Habyarimana's French jet in the eastern sky. But it was no matter. Logic was out the window. The Belgians and the rebels must have worked together. Of course.

A crowd of excited Rwandan soldiers set upon the Belgians and began clubbing them, some of them to death. A few of them managed to grab a loaded rifle and take refuge in a small concrete building near the camp entrance. They managed to fend off their attackers for a terrified hour before their holdout was stormed. They were tortured and mutilated horribly, their tendons sliced so they could not walk.

The secret plan to get the peacekeepers to leave—the one the UN knew about four months in advance—was being carried out according to the letter.

I tried not to listen to RTLM in those first hours, but it could not be avoided. Given the choice between listening to filth and missing potentially crucial information, I will choose the filth every single time.

But it was even worse than I could have imagined. The radio was instructing all its listeners to murder their neighbors.

"Do your work," I heard the announcers say. "Clean your neighborhood of brush. Cut the tall trees."

I would hear variations on these phrases echoing countless times over the next three months. The "tall trees" was an unmistakable reference to the Tutsis. "Clean your neighborhood of brush" meant that rebel army sympathizers might be hiding among Tutsi families and so the entire family should be "cleaned" to be on the safe side. But somehow the worst phrase of all to me was "Do your work." It made killing sound like a responsibility. Like it was the normal thing to do.

Here at last were the bones under the skin. All the anti-Tutsi rhetoric put out on the air over the previous six months had blossomed into what they were now actually saying out loud:

Kill your neighbors. Murder your friends. Do not leave the graves half full. Fantasy had become reality. Theft of life was now mandatory. This seemed to be the consensus of the national village, a sickening version of justice on the grass.

The mass murders were under way in Kigali. The *Interahamwe* militias started setting up some roadblocks, which were often no more than a few bamboo poles set on milk cartons in the road, or sometimes the burned-out hulk of an automobile. Eventually, the roadblocks would be made of human corpses. Every carload of people that came by was subject to a search and a check of those identity papers that listed ethnicity. Those who were found to be Tutsis were dragged to one side and chopped apart with machetes. The Presidential Guard paid visits to the homes of prominent Tutsis, opposition people and wealthy citizens. Doctors were pulled out of their homes and shot in the head. Old women were stabbed in the throat. Schoolchildren were hit on the head with wooden planks and their skulls cracked open on the concrete with the blow of a boot heel. The elderly were thrown down the waste holes of outhouses and buried underneath a cascade of rocks.

Thousands would die that day, the first citizens of what would become a nation of the murdered.

I looked out the next morning at a street that had been transformed.

There was the usual smoky tang of morning mist in the air, the usual dirt street and adobe walls and gray April sky, but it was a scene I could barely recognize. People whom I had known for several years were wearing military uniforms and several were carrying machetes dripping with blood. Quite a few had guns.

There was one in particular who I will call Marcel, though that is not his real name. He worked in a bank. Marcel had a reputation for a gentle approach in a business that can sometimes be hard-hearted. His specialty was helping uneducated people work their way through complicated financial transactions, and I never once knew him to lose his temper. He seemed to be a gentleman who respected himself. But here he was, wearing a military uniform and apparently ready to kill—if he hadn't already.

"Marcel," I remember saying, "I didn't know you were a soldier."

I was trying to keep the irony out of my voice, but he gave me a blank look through his banker's spectacles.

"The enemy is among us," he told me. "The enemy is within us. This is very clear. Many of the people we have been mixing with *are traitors.*"

I thought it best to end the conversation there and went back into my house. Marcel watched me go. I could hear gunfire all around us, though not a heavy concentration from one place, as from a military battle. The rounds were cracking all around periodically, almost lazily, in every direction.

What I did not tell Marcel—what I was not about to tell anybody—was that there were up to thirty-two of the enemy already packed inside my house. These were neighbors who knew they were on the lists of the *Interahamwe*. There was Muhigi and his family, as well as Michel Mugabo. There were also people like me who had refused, for one reason or another, to buy one of the cheap firearms on the street prior to the eruption of mass murder. Why they thought I might be able to protect them was beyond me, but it was my house they flocked to. We put the visitors up in the living room and the kitchen and tried to stay quiet.

It occurred to me later: I had seen this before. My father had opened our tiny hillside home to refugees during the Hutu Revolution of 1959. I had been a young boy then, a little older than my son Tresor. My father's favorite proverb came back to me: "If a man can keep a fierce lion under his roof, why can he not shelter a fellow human being?"

Earlier on that endless morning we had lost track of our son Roger. In the chaos of getting all our frightened visitors comfortable my wife and I had failed to keep a vigilant eye on the children. At the time, Lys was sixteen, Roger was fifteen, Diane was thirteen, and little Tresor was not even two years old. We had instructed them all quite sternly not to go outside under any circumstances, but in the early morning Roger could not resist a check on the welfare of our neighbors. He had gone over the wall, as he would in normal times, to see his next-door friend, a boy who everybody called Rukujuju, which means "boy who sleeps in the ash." I suppose it sounds like a mean thing to call a child, but it was one of those nicknames that must be understood as loving teasing. In any case, the boy never seemed to take offense.

Rukujuju had been hacked apart with a machete. He lay facedown in the backyard in a small pool of his own blood. Nearby lay the bodies of his mother, his six sisters, and two neighbors. Some of them were not yet dead and were moving around slowly. Roger blundered back over the wall and went immediately into his room. He did not speak for the next several days.

These neighbors had joined others who had been slaughtered around us. The woman who lived in the house behind ours was named Leocadia. She was an elderly widow who used to totter over to my house to gossip with Tatiana. Her son was unmarried, a source of some concern for her. She was a Tutsi, but it didn't matter to any of us. Not until today.

I heard the sounds of a commotion at her front door and peered over the wall. There was a band of hyped-up *Interahamwe* there, holding guns and machetes. There was no time to think through my decision. I leaped over the wall and dashed to get help from my neighbor who I knew was a soldier in the Rwandan Army, but not a hardliner.

"Please," I told the soldier who opened the door to me.

"They are going to kill this old woman. Come over and save her." Leocadia was dead, but without any apparent wounds. By the time we arrived with his colleague, it was already too late. She died of a heart attack. I do not want to know what the last thing she saw might have been.

• • •

What was I going to do? It seemed terribly strange to be thinking about work, but my mind kept drifting back to my responsibilities as the general manager of the Hotel Diplomates. It has since been suggested to me that this is one of the ways that people cope with things too horrible to understand—they gladly throw themselves into the little tasks of normal life as a way to distract themselves from the abyss. Perhaps this is what I was doing; I am not sure. But I can tell you that while the corpses of my neighbors stacked up around me I was obsessed with figuring out how to return to the hotel where I felt I belonged. The manager of the nearby Hotel Mille Collines, Bik Cornelis, was a white man and a citizen of the Netherlands who had told me he would almost certainly be evacuated on the first available flight. This would leave not one but two hotels without any leadership during the bloodshed. I had promised the Sabena Corporation that I would do my best to look after both properties when he left. It seemed vital that I live up to my word on this matter. I was apparently useless here at home, anyway.

In the middle of the day on April 7 I finally succeeded in getting through on the telephone with Michel Houtard, the director of the hotels division of the Sabena Corporation. He was a European gentleman of the old landed-gentry school, courtly and generous. He came on the line and I could hear genuine concern in his voice. We had a conversation in French.

"Paul, we are hearing very bad reports of violence breaking out all over Kigali. Are you in any danger?"

"Not at the moment, but I am trapped in my house. Some of my neighbors have been killed. The roads are too dangerous to travel and I have not been able to arrange a military escort to the hotel."

"Can we help in any way?"

"I'm not sure. If I can get to the hotel I will contact you from there and let you know the situation. The radio news has been sketchy. I have to tell you that I am not very well informed about what is going on."

"Well, I want to let you know that we will be trying to do all we can from here to ensure the safety of you and all the employees."

It was strange: While we spoke, I could not help but see the city of Brussels, where Tatiana and I had been just the week before. I pictured flocks of pigeons bobbing their heads in parks, gray mansard roofs, statues of dead aristocrats on horseback, chocolates under glass, pastel-painted town houses, bars full of carefree young people drinking Jupiler pilsner. It had been spring there and the trees were just coming into bud. It seemed like another existence altogether.

I really should have been dead. In retrospect it is a miracle that my name was not on the lists of the undesirables that the Presidential Guard were sent out to eliminate in the first two days. I had been an irritant to Habyarimana and a member of the moderate party. I had been the one who hosted that conference at the Diplomates called by the hated RPF. Furthermore, I was married to a Tutsi "cockroach" and had fathered a baby—my son Tresor—of mixed descent. They had every reason to behead me. Somebody had recently scrawled a number in charcoal on the outer wall of my house—it was 531. I could only guess that it was a code, and an easy way for the death squads to find me.

Every time I saw soldiers walking down my street I assumed it would be my door they would come knocking upon. My plan was to keep working the phones and hope that the military or the UN could find time to get me and my family an escort to the Diplomates. But the radio made it sound as if all hell was breaking loose in Kigali and it was not clear when the troubles would ebb.

On the morning of April 9 they finally came for me. Two Army jeeps tore into my front yard and a squad of soldiers piled out. The captain walked up to me and poked a finger in my face. He was sweating heavily and had angry eyes. I saw immediately that this conversation could very well end with him shooting me in the face. I looked at him with the calmest expression I could manage.

"I hear you are the manager of the Hotel Diplomates," he told me. "We need you to open up the hotel. We want you to come with us."

Here was my chance. I told him I would be happy to accompany him to the hotel, if only my family could come. What I didn't tell him was my extremely liberal interpretation of the word *family*. This was my excuse to load my neighbors and family into the hotel van and my neighbor's car. I would call them my "uncles," "aunts," "nephews," and "nieces" if challenged. I gave my own car keys to another neighbor named Ngarambe.

"This car could save your life," I told him quietly.

We followed the Army caravan on the road out of Kabeza but went only a mile before the captain waved me to pull over at a spot on the road where dead bodies were piled on both sides. It was the scene of a slaughter.

The captain came over to me with a rifle.

"Do you know that all the managers in this country have already been killed?"

"No," I said.

"Even if you do not know, this is how it is. And you, traitor, are lucky we aren't killing you. We have guns and we're going to kill all the cockroaches in the hotel bar and in your house. You are going to help us."

The captain held out the rifle and nodded toward the people huddled in the cars. His message was clear: These people were to be killed right now. And I was chosen to be their killer. It would be my rite of passage.

But I noticed something. *He would not look me in the eye.*

In that one small turn of the face, I saw that there might be some room for me to maneuver. I saw that I had a small chance to save the lives of my family and neighbors. All I needed to do was find the right words. Everything now depended on my words.

I looked at the Kalashnikov rifle this army captain was offering me—bidding me to wipe out the cockroaches like a good patriotic Hutu—and then I began to talk.

"Listen, my friend, I do not know how to handle a gun," I told him. "And even if I did, I do not see what would be accomplished by killing these people."

Surrounding us on every side were the bodies of people who had been freshly murdered. They had been pushed out of the roadway. A few of the lucky ones had been shot, but most had been hacked apart by machetes. Some were missing their heads. I saw the intestines of one man coming out of his belly like pink snakes. This captain had taken me to this spot on the road on purpose, I thought, and was counting on all the bodies and the blood to send a clear message. You will join these corpses if you don't follow our orders, he wanted me to understand. But he would not look me in the eye when he asked me to kill and that's how I understood—somehow—there was a crack in his resolve that I could exploit. I wasn't yet sure how or why, since he and his men could have clearly killed me on the spot without consequence or remorse.

I went over to one of the cars where my neighbors were huddled. I purposely selected the frailest old man I could find and asked the captain: "Look, is *this* really the enemy you are fighting?" I pointed out a baby in a mother's arms, and said it again, trying to push all the panic out of my voice: "Is this baby your enemy? I don't think this is what you want to do. You are what? Twenty-five years old? You are young. Do you want to spend the rest of your life with blood on your hands?"

When I saw this argument wasn't going anywhere, I switched tactics. I aimed lower this time. Morality wasn't working; maybe greed would.

"My friends," I said, "you cannot be blamed for this mistake. I understand you perfectly. You are tired. You are hungry. You are thirsty. This war has stressed you."

I wanted just one thing to leap into his mind: cash. But I wasn't sure this was going to work either. I had only a few minutes to size him up and wasn't sure where his ultimate interests lay. Maybe he was more hardline than I had thought. I found myself wishing I could put a cognac in front of him to loosen him up. Everything now came down to how well I was reading this man—if the promise of money would be enough to tempt him away from the murders he had been ordered to commit. I was like a Mephistopheles trying to corrupt him. It was a role I was only too happy to play if he would only spare the lives of the people behind me.

"I have another solution," I told him. "I know how to solve this problem. Let us talk otherwise."

We began to talk in terms of cash. It seems strange to say, but putting a price on lives was like a kind of sanity compared to the murders he had been suggesting. At first the captain demanded that each Tutsi cockroach pay every one of his soldiers 200,000 Rwandan francs in exchange for their lives. This was roughly the equivalent of $1,500 American per person—many times more cash than an average Rwandan will ever see in their lifetimes. But this was negotiation. You always start with the crazy price and then work downward.

"My friends," I said, "even you do not have this much money. You cannot expect these people to be carrying that kind of sum. But I can get it for you. I am the only person who can do this here. It is in the safe of the hotel and you will never be able to open it without me. Drive me to the hotel and I will pay you the money."

I hustled the refugees into the manager's house of the Diplomates. In a way, we were going straight into the dragon's den—these were the men who were ordering Hutu citizens to pick up kitchen knives and machetes and kill anybody in

Rwanda suspected of being a descendant of the Tutsi clans or one of their allies. But I knew I would be safe here. Despite the captain's bluster, I had sized him up as a basically small man. He would not kill me in the presence of his superiors.

I told the captain to stay where he was—I now felt confident enough to command *him*—and got his money out of the safe. It was the price we had finally agreed on: a million Rwandan francs for everyone. It was the end of the week when we always had a stockpile of liquid cash. It was supposed to have been converted into foreign currency and wired to the corporate office in Belgium. Now it was going into the pockets of killers, but I think it was the best use of that cash anybody could have imagined.

I went and paid off the captain. He drove away with his death squad and I never saw him again.

It was later suggested to me that I could have broken my agreement with this killer, simply refusing to pay the money once I and my neighbors and family were safely inside the Diplomates. But this was inconceivable. He would have remembered me and surely taken revenge, for one thing. And I had given him my word. Even if it was loathsome to reward him for being a potential killer and to measure human lives in cash, I never make promises I cannot keep. It is bad policy. There is a saying in Rwanda: With a lie you can eat once, but never twice.

He left me with something valuable, too. He told me that I was not powerless in the face of the murderous insanity that seemed to have descended over my country in the last seventy-two hours.

With that brief refusal to meet my eyes, he told me that I might be able to negotiate with evil.

I soon discovered the true reason why I had been brought to the Diplomates and not killed. It was solely because of the keys I had been holding. The interim government of Rwanda—a rump committee of the very same men who had organized the militias—had taken over all the rooms as a temporary headquarters of the new government. But they needed the keys. Once I had opened the suites and the bar, my life was expendable. I tried my best to keep myself and my family out of sight and they seemed to forget about me in the chaos, for which I was deeply grateful.

The rebels soon learned what was happening at the Diplomates and started firing mortar shells at the hotel, which was all too exposed on the hillside. They had an easy shot from their stronghold near the Parliament building. Bullets started whizzing through the windows and I couldn't go into my office because it faced the direction of fire. The crisis government hastily started packing supplies and papers into boxes and prepared to decamp to the city of Gitarama, about fifty kilometers southwest. They also looted bedspreads, pillows, television sets, and other items from their rooms, but it seemed best not to complain about this small larceny. There was my own life to think about. I made a show of preparing to evacuate with them and they seemed not to mind—although what they would want with a hotel manager I have no idea.

It did not matter: I had a secret plan in mind. My family and I would pretend to follow the military train, but then split off almost immediately. We would use the cover of the government convoy as a safe way to get to Sabena's other luxury property, the Hotel Mille Collines. This was a place I knew very well from my time there in the 1980s and there were four hundred refugees who had taken shelter there. Barely a half mile of hillside separated the two properties; I could have walked it in ten minutes during peaceful times. But it would have been inviting death by machete to do it now while the *Interahamwe* were running about. We would have to leave my neighbors hidden inside the cottage—it was too dangerous to try to move them out now—but I resolved not to forget them. I would simply have to come back later and rescue them by other means. But I wasn't sure I could even save my family, or myself. I would be leaving the Diplomates, where I was technically still the manager, and going over to the Mille Collines, where I had plenty of friends and a long work history but was technically not the boss. What kind of reception was I going to get over there? I had no idea what would happen.

On the morning of April 12 the government leaders started their trip to the emergency capital and I rolled out with them behind the wheel of a Suzuki jeep. On that brief five-minute trip I kept seeing patches of red on the dirt of the shoulder. Days later I would see trucks that would normally have been used to haul concrete blocks or other construction material. They would be stacked high with dead bodies: women, men, children, many of them with stumps where their arms and legs had been. Somebody with the city sanitation department apparently had the foresight to clean them off the roadways and take them for burial in mass graves all over Kigali.

For now, though, there were only the bloodstains on the side of the road. "Don't look," I said to my children and my wife. But I had to keep my eyes open to drive.

SIX

I PEELED AWAY from the killers and turned the car toward my beloved Hotel Mille Collines.

A squad of militia had set up a roadblock right in front of the entrance. I had come to dread them on sight—young boys, many no older than fourteen, dressed in ragged clothes with red, green, and yellow stripes and carrying spears and machetes and a few battered rifles. These boys had liberated some Primus beer from someplace and were guzzling it down, though it was early in the morning. They were checking the identification papers of everyone attempting to get inside the Mille Collines. But they had not yet entered the hotel itself.

I got out of the car to talk to them. It is always better to be face-to-face with the man you intend to deal with rather than have him standing over you. To be on the same physical plane changes the tone of the conversation.

"I'm the manager of both the Diplomates and the Mille Collines," I told them. "I'm coming to see what is going on."

To my surprise they did not ask me for my identification

book. They glanced briefly at my family in the car before waving us through. I thought I saw them smirk to each other. If I had to guess what they were thinking, it would be this: "Oh, why not let six more cockroaches inside? It will make it easier to find them when the time comes." They looked at me and my wife and children and must have seen corpses.

All over Rwanda people were leaving their homes and running to places where they thought they might be spared.

Churches were favorite hiding places. In the village of Ntarama just south of the capital the mayor told the local population of Tutsis to go inside the rectangular brick Catholic church to wait out the violence instead of trying to hide in the nearby swamps. The church had been a safe refuge during the troubles in 1959 and nobody had forgotten the seemingly magical role that it had played. More than five thousand frightened people crammed inside. But here, as well as every-where in Rwanda, the sanctuaries of Christ were a cruel trap; they only made easy places for the mobs to herd the fugitives. RTLM radio kept saying the churches were staging bases and weapons depots for the rebel invaders, which was total nonsense, but it provided a motivation—and perhaps some intellectual comfort—for hesitant killers to go inside and start chopping. Like my father said when I was a boy: "Any excuse will serve a tyrant."

Four busloads of cheerful Army soldiers and militiamen arrived to do the job at Ntarama. A man named Aphrodise Nsengiyumva was at the altar leading prayers and trying to keep everyone cheerful when those outside started breaking holes through the walls with sledgehammers and grenades. Light streamed into the darkened room. It would be among the last things most people in here would ever see. Grenades were tossed in through the holes, blasting some of the refugees into bits, splashing blood and muscle tissue all over the compound. Other militiamen broke down the doors and waded into the crowd with spears, clubs, and machetes. Babies were ripped from their mother's arms and dashed against the wall. People were cut down as they prayed.

It happened at secular buildings as well, and there, too, death was usually preceded by a betrayal.

A rumor went around in the suburb of Kicukiro, for example, that the UN troops stationed at a technical school would offer protection from the mobs. There were indeed ninety commandos at the school, but they were less than eager to offer any protection. Nonetheless, about two thousand of the hunted took shelter in the classroom buildings behind the very thin layer of safety afforded by the blue helmets and their weapons.

On April 12, the same day my family and I reached the Mille Collines, the order was given for the UN troops to abandon the school and help make sure that foreigners got out of Rwanda safely. The mission had changed. As the country slid further and further into mass murder, the Security Council, Kofi Annan, and the United States decided that the mandate of the UN troops was not to halt the killings but to ensure an orderly evacuation of all non-Rwandans. Everyone else was to be left behind. Anyone with white skin or a foreign passport was given a free trip out. Even their pet dogs were evacuated with them.

The nation of Belgium was more than happy to go along; the grisly torture slayings of the ten soldiers assigned to protect Prime Minister Agathe Uwilingiyimana had shocked the public back home. The former colonial masters could no longer stomach the quagmire they had helped create. As it happened, the ninety UN troops at the vocational school were native Belgians. They must have heard the stories of the militia at the roadblocks making sawing motions across their throats with machetes whenever they spotted a Belgian uniform. Most of the *Interahamwe,* in fact, would be given standing orders to kill any person found carrying a Belgian passport. The militias surrounding the school did not have the firepower to take on the UN soldiers, so they lay on the grass drinking beer and chanting slogans and making threatening gestures. It must have been something of a relief for those Belgian soldiers to move out, knowing they would be killed cheerfully if they ran out of ammunition in a firefight. This was the clearest signal yet that the world was preparing to close its eyes, close its ears, and turn its back on what was happening.

The refugees knew what lay in store. Some begged the departing soldiers to shoot them in the head so they would not have to face slow dismemberment. Others tried to lie down in front of the Belgians' jeeps so they could not leave. Still others chased after the vehicles screaming, "Do not abandon us!" The soldiers responded by shooing the refugees out of the way and firing warning shots to keep them from mobbing the departing convoy.

The massacre of two thousand people began immediately after the last UN jeep had disappeared down the street.

I decided to get rid of that roadblock outside the hotel. It was a danger to everyone inside the Mille Collines. Anybody trying to come inside would have to show their identity book. Those who could not prove their Hutuness would be murdered on the spot, barely fifty yards from temporary refuge.

After I made sure that my wife and children were safely behind the doors of Room 126 I retreated into the manager's office with what would turn out to be one of the most formidable weapons I had in my possession. Its existence was kept secret from just about everybody I knew. It was taken out only in moments of complete privacy.

It was a black leather binder that I had purchased many years ago on a trip to Belgium. Inside were about a hundred pages of closely written script, arranged in three columns on each page. There were entries for name, for title, and for phone number.

This was my personal directory of numbers for the elite circle of government and commerce in Rwanda. For years I had made a habit of collecting the business cards of local people who passed through the Diplomates or the Mille Collines and then entering their information in pencil in my binder at the end of the day. If they came into the hotel often enough, and if I liked them, I made sure that they occasionally received little gifts from me. Almost everyone in this book had a favorite drink and I tried to keep that information memorized. If I heard gossip that a particular person had been demoted, promoted, transferred, fired, or jailed I made a change to their title. Army officers, managers, doctors, ministers, professors— they were all listed in neat phalanxes, and the eraser marks and crossed-out titles next to their names were a rough map of the shifting sands of Rwandan politics. My binder may have been one of the better registries of power in the capital. I could never be certain about this, of course, because nobody would talk about keeping such a thing. It could be used as evidence if you were found to be connected to a person who fell from grace.

Now, of course, I had no idea who in this book was still in power—or even alive.

Many of the lines rang without anybody picking up. There were a handful of busy signals and quite a few tonal patterns that indicated phones were out of service. But then I found myself talking to a young military camp chief named, as it happened, Commander Habyarimana, though he was not related to the assassinated president. After a few minutes of conversation, I began to recall what I had heard about him, and I realized that I had come to the right place. The commander was an angry young man, but not for the same reasons that the *Interahamwe* were angry. His fury was directed at the presidential cronies, who he felt were responsible for turning Rwanda into an armed hothouse of people who hated one another for no good reason. Commander Habyarimana had wound up on the wrong end of a dispute with a superior and had been thrown into Kigali's notorious jail for political prisoners, which was nicknamed "1930" for its year of construction. He was eventually released and had been able to climb back up the military ladder. He was just as disgusted as I was at the recent outbreaks of murder, and he promised to send me five of his men to help protect the hotel from invasion.

It was a good start, but I still wanted that roadblock gone.

I made a few more calls and finally got on the line with General Augustin Ndindiliyimana, a man whom I had known for several years. He was the commander of the National Police. I did not envy him his position. The army had drafted thousands of his best officers and appropriated a large part of the police arsenal, leaving him with a squad of, at most, a thousand poorly trained and unequipped recruits to get control of the violent capital streets. Whatever he could do for me was going to be a major gift.

"Now, general," I said quietly, in the voice of a man calling in a chip. "We have some refugees over here, as you know, and that militia outside can come inside here anytime they want."

I knew that he was afraid of the *Interahamwe* himself, and perhaps also of being accused of not supporting the pogroms that had recently become the law of the land. It seemed that such a perception could spell death in these times. But I kept at him.

"General, you know we are friends and will always be friends. You know that I would not ask this if I weren't in great danger. Something must be done about that roadblock. You could send some officers to encourage those boys to move elsewhere. There doesn't need to be bloodshed in front of my hotel."

It continued on like this for a while, and he agreed he would help me. I wasn't certain if he was going to come through. But within a few hours the roadblock had disappeared.

Having won that temporary respite, I turned my attention to another problem. I had to get hold of the master keys that opened everything in the hotel. These were the tools that a hotel manager cannot afford to be without.

Bik Cornelis had told me that he had entrusted the keys to the reception staff, and so I approached one of the supervisors there, a man I'll call Jacques.

"Hello," I said. "It is now my responsibility to look after the hotel. I understand you have the keys?"

"Ah yes, the keys," he said. "I am not sure who has them right now."

He made a show of asking his associate, who also denied any direct knowledge of their whereabouts. But these men had charge of the reception desk, which is where Bik had told me the keys could be found. It was immediately clear what was really happening, although neither Jacques nor I felt any need to say it outright.

I should pause here and explain what I mean. Despite its history of bloodshed and jealousy Rwandan culture is rooted in an attitude of excessive politeness. Perhaps it comes from all the fear in our background, the heavy hand of the European masters pressed down on our ancestors, but nobody here likes to give a simple no. It is viewed as rude. So what you often get in response to a direct question is a rambling story in which the refusal is voiced through a very soft yes. Or you often get an outright lie. Important conversations can turn into exhausting set pieces. Ask an average Rwandan on the street where he is going that day, and he'll be likely to tell you "Oh, I don't really know," even though he knows very well. Elusive answers are a national art form; any man on the street here could easily work as a high-level diplomat. But both parties usually know what is being said without anyone having to say it out loud. We call this "the

Rwandan no." Occasionally it can be misread. But I was almost certain that Jacques was blowing smoke because he liked the idea of being in charge of the Mille Collines.

I soon found out that he was staying in the manager's apartment with his girlfriend. He was also giving orders to the staff as though he was in charge of the hotel. He had taken several bottles of the best champagne and was having a party with his friends. I did not view this as an affront to my pride so much as I viewed it as a threat to my life and the lives of the refugees upstairs. I had no idea where his loyalties really lay. We were in danger of invasion and slaughter and I suspected that he was informing the thugs outside of what was happening in here and who was occupying what room. But I could not fire him without risking a staff coup d'état at this fragile time.

I got on the phone to the Sabena Corporation in Brussels to clarify that I had their support. I then asked them to fax me a letter naming me the interim manager of the Mille Collines until further notice. It came rolling through a few seconds later, bearing the signature of Michel Houtard. He always joked that I might become president of Rwanda, but for now I just wanted to take control of this hotel for a few more days, until the danger had passed.

Photocopies of the letter were immediately tacked onto employee bulletin boards all over the property. And then I went to Jacques again. This time there was no pretense of cordiality.

"I want the keys *right now*," I told him. "And I want this

place in good order. If you agree with me, fine. If you don't, then, please: good-bye." I got my keys.

There were two main reasons why the Hotel Mille Collines was left alone in those early days even while churches and schools became abattoirs.

The first was the initial confusion—and even timidity—of the militias. Raiding the hotel would have been a fairly high-profile operation and one that surely would have angered a lot of people in power. The Mille Collines had an image of being linked with the ruling elite and was viewed as something not to be tampered with. This mind-set was not set in stone, however, and I'm sure it would have changed as the genocide wore on and the killers grew bolder.

The second reason we were able to get some breathing room is one I have already mentioned. We had five policemen standing outside thanks to my new friend, Commander Habyarimana. As fragile as this protection was, it was still much better than what we got from the UN, which amounted to just about nothing. They had a force of 2,700 troops stationed in Rwanda when the president was assassinated, and the majority of them had been evacuated along with all the foreigners. But about 500 peacekeepers were to be left in the country—God knows why—and 4 of them were staying as guests at the Mille Collines. They were well meaning but useless.

On April 16 I sent General Dallaire a letter informing him of our situation and asking him for some additional soldiers to safeguard our refugees. I heard later that he ordered the Bangladeshis to come help us but that their commander flat-out refused. Dallaire then rescinded his order. This was appalling to me, and I was not even a military man. This incident underlined what a later United Nations report termed "grave problems of command and control" within the mission and heightened my feeling that Dallaire could have and should have done more to put his men in between the killers and their victims.

This is not a condemnation of Romeo Dallaire as a person. I always liked him and felt he had a compassionate heart and a strong sense of morality. He had acted with honor and determination under extremely bad circumstances—and with a shameful lack of support from his bosses on the UN staff and on the Security Council. Early in the genocide he had insisted that with just five thousand well-equipped soldiers he could have stopped the killings, and nobody has ever doubted his judgment. Dallaire had also proved himself to be a shrewd commander of the media during the crisis, granting multiple radio interviews in an attempt to get the world to pay attention to what was happening here. I would gladly share a cognac with him today, and I would hope we could also share a laugh. But I still feel he should have disobeyed his foolish orders from New York and acted more aggressively to stop street murders from taking place.

There is no doubt he would have taken more casualties and turned the UN into a third belligerent in the civil war, but I am convinced this action would have slapped the world in the face and forced it to do something about the unspeakable carnage here. At the very least it would have forced the UN to beef up its peacekeeping force and send us real fighters instead of inept draftees from nations who seemed more interested in collecting their per diem payments from the UN instead of doing anything meaningful.

If he did not have the stomach to do this then I think he should have made a spectacle out of resigning in protest of his hopeless job description. This, too, would have drawn some outrage to what was shaping up to be the most rapid genocide in world history. That he stayed in his job like a good soldier was a signal of a trust that the UN strategy of nonengagement was going to be a workable policy even though it appears despicable in retrospect.

In my opinion the UN was not just useless during the genocide. It was *worse* than useless. It would have been better off for us if they did not exist at all, because it allowed the world to think that something was being done, that some parental figure was minding the store. It created a fatal illusion of safety. Rwanda was left with a little more than five hundred poorly trained UN soldiers who weren't even authorized to draw their weapons to stop a child from being sacrificed right in front of them. A total withdrawal would have been preferable to this farce.

The grounds of the Mille Collines were surrounded by a fence of bamboo and wire. It was about six feet high and intended by the architect to provide a visual sense of a snug compound, all the better for nervous foreign visitors to feel like their hotel was an island of safety embedded in the street grid of Kigali. If you pushed on the fence hard enough it would fall over. It provided an illusion of protection, nothing more.

From the corridor windows of the west wing, and from some of the room balconies, you could see over the top of this fence and also through the gaps. There were figures passing back and forth all day long on the other side, like backstage players making shadows on a curtain. Most were carrying spears and machetes. Some stopped to peer at us through the fence before moving on.

All the refugees, including my wife and children, were terrified of these shadows behind the bamboo. Tatiana's family was living in a small town near the city of Butare, where the killings had not yet started but were imminent. She was terrified for them, terrified for herself and our children and me, and I cannot say I blame her. Everyone in the hotel felt a similar sense of dread. I felt terribly exposed here, but I did not see an alternative. If we left it would be a sign to the killers that the Mille Collines was being surrendered. Besides, where else could we go? Nowhere in Rwanda was safe.

This belief of mine was the subject of a bitter fight between us. My wife confronted me in the parking lot and insisted we drive to safety in my home area of Murama. To back up her argument she enlisted my friend Aloise Karasankwavu, an executive with the Commercial Bank who was also in fear of his life. He was a persuasive speaker, and we jousted .

"In all of history there has never been a war brought to that little town," he told me. And in a sense he was right—at least in my own memory. The uprisings of 1959 and 1973 had created a lot of prejudice in my hometown, but they had never resulted in massacres. But there was no guarantee that blood wasn't being spilled there right now, without our knowledge.

"My friend, the whole country has gone mad," I told him. "Do you think Murama will be spared?"

"You are being misled by the Europeans, Paul. Even the *mwami* used to bring his cows there for safekeeping during times of trouble. Throughout history it has always been a refuge."

"Aloise, even if that were true, how do you think you are going to get there? By flying? There are hundreds of roadblocks out there. You will be stopped and possibly killed."

I looked at my wife, whose eyes were red and miserable. I only wished we had stayed in Brussels a week ago. I wanted to go to Murama as badly as she did—I still had brothers and sisters living there and I was tremendously worried for them—but I knew it would be risking death to go out onto the roads.

I am not necessarily proud of what I did next, but it happened. I lost my temper.

"Listen," I told her, "you have a driver's license. You know how to drive."

I held out the keys to the Suzuki jeep.

"Take these," I told her. "*You* go to Murama."

She looked back at me with furious eyes. We loved each other fiercely, but she was a Tutsi and I was a Hutu. This trivia of ancestry had never mattered the slightest bit in our marriage, but it mattered to the killers around us, and I loathed Rwanda more than I ever had before because of it. Once again I hated myself for being a lucky Hutu. Many years before Tatiana's father had taken the precaution of changing the whole family's identification cards to read "Hutu," but she might have been recognized by someone at a roadblock. We both knew this.

I was, of course, not going to surrender the keys to my wife under any circumstances. I only wanted to make a point. But it was a harsh one, and perhaps too harsh. I was trying to highlight our need to stay where we were and wait for the bloodletting to stop. But my wife was hurt by my words.

Aloise later took his wife and children and hitched a ride out of town, trying to get to Murama. He did not make five kilometers. The militia forced them all out of the car and separated him from his family. Amazingly, nobody was killed.

Aloise went on foot to the village of Nyanza, and later on to Murama.

I would learn it was extremely fortunate that we decided not to leave the capital.

The Mille Collines grew more and more crowded. The rumor had spread through town that the hotel was a safe haven from the killers. This was far from the truth, but hope becomes a kind of insanity in times of trouble. Those cunning or lucky enough to dodge the roadblocks were welcomed inside, even though the hotel stood every chance of becoming a killing zone without warning.

We charged no money for rooms. All the usual rules were irrelevant; we were now more of a refugee camp than a hotel. To take cash away from anyone would also be to strip them of money they might need to bribe their way out of being murdered. Some guests of mine who were wealthy came to me with a proposal that they would sign a letter of guarantee promising to pay Sabena when the trouble was over, and I accepted this. But nobody was asked for money.

One exception to this rule was liquor. Those who could afford it were allowed to buy cocktails and bottles of beer—never invite a man without one, even in a crisis—and I used the proceeds to help buy food. It was one way of passing the hat. I also asked my bosses at Sabena to send me more cash and they were able to smuggle two hundred thousand Rwandan francs to me with the help of a humanitarian organization that I should not name here. Room, however, was our greatest asset, and one that could not have a price tag attached. I guarded it closely and had to fight for it on one occasion. I have already mentioned my battle with the reception staff. One of them—Jacques, my problem employee—had taken it upon himself to live in the manager's apartment with his girlfriend. They were in there alone, and wasting crucial space. Other recalcitrant employees had followed his example and were claiming the choicest suites for themselves. In my mind, nobody had this prerogative. We needed to conserve and share everything we had, and that included the most precious thing we had to offer.

So I went to their room and knocked. "I have two choices for you," I said. "Either you can move to smaller rooms or you can have some new neighbors." After that I felt free to assign other refugees to sleep in the rooms they had been hogging for themselves. That put a quick end to their party. It also freed up yet more accommodations for those people who kept finding their way to the Mille Collines from the mayhem outside the fence. I resolved that nobody who could make it here would be turned away.

I cannot say that life was normal inside that crowded building, but what I saw in there convinced me that ordinary human beings are born with an extraordinary ability to fight evil with decency. We had Hutu and Tutsi sleeping beside each other. Strangers on the floor, many of whom had witnessed their families being butchered, would sometime sleep spoon style just to feel the touch of another.

We struggled to preserve routines. It helped keep us sane. The bishop from St. Michael's parish, a man named Father Nicodem, was one of our guests and he started holding regular masses in the ballroom. There was no such thing as privacy, but occasionally the occupants of a room would clear out to give a husband and a wife some room to make love. Several women became pregnant during the genocide, a way of fighting death with life, I suppose.

There was even a wedding. A seventeen-year-old girl was pregnant and her father was a very traditional Muslim who wanted nothing more than to see her married so the child would not be born outside wedlock. The bishop agreed to perform the sacrament in the ballroom. She was married right there to her boyfriend, and nobody thought to question the difference in faiths.

I suppose it is natural to want a form of government, even in times of chaos (perhaps *especially* in times of chaos), and so five of the guests agreed to serve as a kind of high council to mediate disputes between the residents. I met regularly with them as a sort of chairman. You might have called the Hotel Mille Collines a kind of constitutional monarchy in those days, because I reserved the right to make all the final judgments on matters of day-to-day living. My kingship came not from a heavenly birthright but from the personnel department of the Sabena Corporation sent via fax from Brussels.

In mid-April we lost our water and electricity. The killers had cut all of our utility lines in an attempt to make us uncomfortable. Perhaps they thought we would all drift away and then they could finish us off outside. It confirmed for me what I already knew—that they had designs to murder us—but it also gave me a bit of hope. The militia still did not want to risk an overt massacre at the hotel. We ran our emergency generator for a while with smuggled gasoline, but it eventually broke down, and so most of our time was spent in darkness.

Life immediately became even harder. The absence of electric lights created a mood I can only describe as disintegrating. How secure those lights had somehow made us feel! Everybody knew the killers liked to do their work in the dark, and the darkness inside the hotel made it feel like a permanent midnight. The absence of light created a sense of decay around the world, which appeared to be running down on its axis, its center breaking apart into mindless pieces. Our last days would be spent in shadows.

Each room held an average of eight frightened and brutalized people. They slept fitfully in the humid dark and often awoke to the sounds of a neighbor shouting or whimpering in a dream. There were mothers who cried out for sons who they would never see again, husbands who wept in secret for their disappeared wives. And though few people wanted to say it out loud, I think most shared my belief that we would all wind up dead ourselves when the militias outside finally decided to raid the Mille Collines. Those hotel rooms were like death-row prison cells, but we knew they were all that kept us from joining the ranks of the murdered for one more day. I worried there would be no more space, but we kept finding ways to fit more people inside our walls. I suppose it is like the story of the oil not running out in the Temple of Jerusalem. There was always more room. I think I would have ordered my guests to start lying on top of one another if it would have meant saving a few more lives. And I don't think anybody inside the Mille Collines would have objected.

That these people crammed together in the rancid half light, each nursing their own horrors, could endure such conditions and keep on fighting on the side of life is proof to me not just of the human capacity for endurance but also to the basic decency inside all people that comes out when death appears imminent. To me, that old saying about one's life flashing before the eyes is really a love for *all* life in those final moments and not merely one's own; a primal empathy for *all* people who are born and must taste death. We clung to one another while the violence escalated, and most of us did not lose faith that order would be restored. Whether we would be there to see it was a separate question. All we could do was wait in the dark, with militia spies coming in and going out at all hours, even sleeping among us like fellow refugees. Cats and mice were in the same cage.

The loss of our utilities created another problem. Without water we would all start to dehydrate, forcing people to go out onto the streets rather than die of thirst. We had only a few days to figure out a solution. Every large compound in Rwanda—embassies, restaurants, and hotels—must have their own set of reserve water tanks built onto the property as an emergency supply. Ours were located directly under the basement. I went to check their levels several times a day and watched them steadily dropping. There was no way to get a fresh delivery.

The solution came to me: We *did* have a reserve supply of water. In the swimming pool.

This pool was, in some ways, the most important part of the Mille Collines. Built in 1973 when the hotel was still new, it was smaller than Olympic size, but it got a lot of use from our European guests who brought children. The logo of the hotel—five overlapping triangles that represented hills—was painted on the slope that led from the deep end to the shallow end. A very ordinary looking pool altogether, but it was the centerpiece of the back lawn, and it was surrounded with ten tables where waiters used to bring cocktails, peanuts, and bar food. This was where the power brokers of Kigali often came to have private conversations with each other in the evening. You never invite a man without a beer.

Something about human nature compels us to draw close to the edge of water. I feel it myself even though I never saw the ocean—or even a lake of any size—until I was seventeen years old. I cannot explain it, but it is real. The tables near the pool were snapped up first, even by men who would not dream of taking a dip, and who may not have been able to swim. Those tables probably saw as much intrigue in the early 1990s as the courtyards of the doge's palace in the heyday of Venice. In any case, that pool was now a tool of life.

Here was the math. It held approximately seventy-eight thousand gallons. At the time, we had nearly eight hundred guests. If we limited each person to a gallon and a half a day for their washing and drinking needs we could last for a little longer than two months. A rationing system would have to be devised so that each person could be insured of receiving a fair share. So we began a twice-daily ritual: Every morning at 8:30 and every afternoon at 5:00 everyone was told to come down with the small plastic wastepaper bin from their room. They were allowed to dip it once into the pool water, which was already turning slightly yellow. In order to keep the water as clean as possible, we did not permit anyone to swim in it, or even to wade.

The room toilets no longer flushed, and so we had to devise a method to get rid of waste. One of the guests discovered a trick, which was quickly broadcast to the hotel at large: If you poured the pool water into the commode it would still wash the feces and the urine down the pipes. The rooms began to smell a little worse, but at least there was no imminent sanitary emergency.

As for food, we were well stocked at first. Before the massacres started Sabena had a limited partnership with its rival Air France on the question of catering meals for passengers. Because the hotel was the property of the airline their ready-to-eat meals were stored in the basement of the hotel. We did a count: There were approximately two thousand trays. Those would be a limited luxury that we parceled out stingily. It was very strange, of course, to be dining on rosemary chicken and potatoes au gratin while young boys with machetes in hand peered at us over the bamboo fence.

When the airline meals ran low we had to come up with an alternate plan. Even though there were senseless murders happening all over the country—more than five every minute—the marketplaces were still open. People still had to shop, even in the middle of a genocide. I sent the hotel accountant, a man named Belliad, out with a truck and some cash to get us sacks of corn and beans and bundles of firewood. We tried to acquire rice and potatoes, but they were unavailable. I then asked the kitchen staff to cook it up. Since they had no electricity to run the stoves and ovens we had to build a fire underneath the giant ficus tree on the lawn. Large pots of food were set in the blaze. We then served up this vegetable gruel in the large metal trays we had used for buffet-style meals on the lawn. We ate as a group twice a day, the hotel's fine china balanced on our laps. If the pool was now a village well, the lawn was now our cookhouse.

Now that was a sight! It used to be that we would use the back lawn to host weddings, conferences, and diplomatic receptions. I remembered nights out here with men in dark suits tailored in London and women in long silk dresses, holding cocktails in thin-stemmed glasses, their faces gently lit with the soft colors of Malibu lights and their laughter like the music of an opera libretto. Now our party was one of exhausted refugees in dirty clothes, some with machete wounds, many who had seen their friends turn into killers and their family turned into corpses, all lined up under the ficus tree for that simple act of eating that unconsciously signifies a small piece of hope, the willingness to store up fuel and keep living for another day.

SEVEN

WE LOST OUR PHONE SERVICE near the end of April. This was potentially disastrous. Without a phone my black binder would be nearly useless. I could no longer call in favors with the Army brass or the government.

But then came a surprise. In 1987, when I was the assistant general manager, the Mille Collines received its first fax machine. We had to request an auxiliary phone line to support it, one that was not routed through the main switchboard. We had asked the technician to feed the fax line directly into the telephone grid of Kigali. This was a glitch I recalled when I was in the darkness of the secretary's office on the day the phones were cut. I was moved to pick up the handset attached to the side of the fax. There was a dial tone humming back at me, as beautiful a sound as I could have imagined.

I guarded this secret carefully. If the hard-liners in the military found out that I had a phone, they would send in their thugs to find it and rip it out. So I let only the refugee committee use it and instructed them to keep quiet. The news could reach the ears of some of my renegade employees, which would be just like telling the *Interahamwe* themselves. I took to locking the door of the secretary's office whenever I was away so that unauthorized people could not wander in and discover my secret weapon. That phone was a lifeline.

I started staying up late at night, often until 4:00 A.M., sending faxes to the Belgian Foreign Ministry, the White House, the United Nations, the Quai d'Orsay, the Peace Corps—whoever I thought might be able to help stop an attack against the hotel. I tried to make the faxes brief and direct and forceful. I described the lack of food, the militia roaming outside, the desperate struggle of refugees to get into the hotel, the constant rumors that we were about to be invaded. I pleaded with these governments and agencies for some kind of assistance and protection. These letters were usually followed by a direct appeal via the little phone handset on the side. But I often felt as though I was a man shouting into an empty room.

One follow-up call to a White House staffer was typical. It was very late at night in Rwanda and the conversation went approximately like this:

"Yes, hello, my name is Paul Rusesabagina. I am the manager of the Hotel Mille Collines in the capital of Rwanda. I sent a fax today to the number your secretary gave me. I was calling to see if you received it."

"Ah, yes, Mr. Roos . . . Roossuhbaggian. How did you get this number?"

"I asked for you at the switchboard."

"I see. You're calling from Rwanda?"

"Yes, Rwanda."

"Yes, I remember the fax. I passed it along to a colleague of mine who handles foreign policy details. He will review it and get back to you."

"So you didn't have a chance to read it? I was told you were the one to handle this matter."

"No, that wouldn't be me. This has to be routed through proper channels. Have you also contacted the State Department or the embassy of the United States in Rwanda?"

"Your embassy left the country on April 9."

"Yes, that's right. I see."

"I was really hoping you could bring this up with President Clinton directly. The situation here is very bad."

"Well, as I have said, this has to be handled by the foreign policy staff. All I can say is that they will review the document and get back to you."

"Who on that staff has been given my letter?"

"I can't really say for sure. I've got another call coming in and I have to let you go."

To all the faxes and phone calls I made to the United States in those weeks, I never once received a reply. It shouldn't have surprised me. I should have known a Rwandan no when I heard one.

On April 26 Thomas Kamilindi, who was one of the city's best journalists, gave a telephone interview to Radio France International in which he described the living conditions at the hotel, the lack of water, and the state of the ongoing genocide and civil war. He also described the rebel advance on the capital. The interview was intended for listeners in Paris and all over the French-speaking world, but it was also broadcast in Kigali.

Apparently some of the *génocidaires* had torn themselves away from RTLM long enough to listen, because there was a death order out for Thomas within the half hour.

Friends in the military urged him to sneak out of the hotel and find another place to hide, but I urged him not to leave. I had been in touch with General Bizimungu and General Dallaire about his situation. We had him switch rooms to fool any spies who might have known where he was staying. Some of the refugees were terribly unhappy with Thomas for focusing attention on the Mille Collines—they thought he only reminded the militia thugs that we were here, dancing just out of their reach. Some of the guests wanted to hand Thomas over as a kind of peace offering to the militia. I couldn't decide if I found this idea abhorrent or laughable.

A friend of Thomas's was sent to the hotel that day to assassinate him. His name was Jean-Baptiste Iradukunda and he was with an Army intelligence unit. They had known each other since they were children. Thomas was smart enough to boldly step out into the corridor and meet his would-be killer face-to-face. They started to talk. I am convinced that had Thomas tried to cower—or worse, to run—that he would have been shot. It is so much easier to die anonymously; it is so much harder to kill someone after you have talked as one human being to another.

"Listen, Thomas," said the solider after a while. "I have been sent to kill you. But I cannot. I am going to leave now. But somebody else will be coming later and they will not be as hesitant."

Immediately after Thomas gave the interview, an Army colonel called from the hotel entrance. He was a man I had known for a long time. I went out to say hello, and he wasted no time telling me what he was there to do.

"Paul, I am here to pick up that dog!"

"You are fighting against a dog, colonel?" I asked him with a small laugh. "Let's go talk about this."

We went back to my office and I asked a chambermaid to bring us drinks. Sitting in the quiet, and without an audience to encourage him, I could already see that some of the rage had leaked away from his countenance. But he remained adamant: He was going to have the head of Thomas Kamilindi.

The interview he had given was an act of treason against the government of Rwanda and the Army.

I began to think that the government leaders were most concerned that they had been embarrassed in front of their French patrons. That they should have cared about an interview describing people drinking from the swimming pool at a time when murder-by-machete was the law of the land tells you something about their mentality. But regardless, the execution order against Thomas was real and I resolved to save his life by any means I could.

I tried flattery first.

"Colonel," I began, "you are too high ranking an officer to be concerned with such a small matter. Thomas is a small man."

"I have orders, Paul."

"You have orders to kill a dog? That is an insulting job. Don't you have boys in the militia who are supposed to do that kind of work?"

"It is not a small matter. He is a traitor and must pay."

I could see that I was getting somewhere, but I switched my argument.

"Listen, colonel. Let's say you take that dog out with your own hands and kill him. You will have to live with that for the rest of your life. You did not hear this radio interview. You do not know what was said. You are proposing to take a man's life without a trial."

"Paul, I have my orders. Where is he?"

"Even if you were to order it done instead of doing it yourself, it would be the same blood on your hands."

It went on like this for quite some time. I don't know why he kept talking to me. But the longer he sat there and sipped his Carlsberg the greater the odds were that Thomas was going to survive to see the sun go down.

"Listen," I finally told him, after more than two hours had gone by, "this war has made everyone a little bit crazy. It is understandable. You are tired. You need to relax. I have some good red wine in the cellar. Let me bring you a carton. I will have it loaded into your jeep. Go home tonight and have a drink and we will talk more about this tomorrow, when we can come to a compromise."

Everything I suggested came to pass—almost. I did find some red wine from the cellar to spare. I had it loaded into his military jeep. So far as I know, he did go home and enjoy some of it that night. But the compromise never happened. The colonel did not come back and Thomas was not executed.

I had dozens of conversations like this throughout the genocide, surreal exchanges in which I would find myself sitting across a desk or a cocktail table with a man who might have committed dozens of killings that day. In several cases I saw flecks of blood on their uniforms or work shirts. We would talk as though nothing was out of the ordinary, as if we were negotiating the purchase of new kitchen equipment or discussing an upcoming special event in the ballroom. Human lives almost always hung in the balance during these talks. But they were always lubricated with beer or cognac, and usually ended with my gifting that day's murderer with a bottle of French champagne or whatever else I could dig out of my dwindling liquor cabinet.

I have since thought a great deal about how people are able to maintain two attitudes in their minds at once. Take the colonel: He had come fresh from a world of machetes, road gangs, and random death and yet was able to have a civilized conversation with a hotel manager over a glass of beer and let himself be talked out of committing another murder. He had a soft side and a hard side and neither was in absolute control of his actions. It would have been dangerous to assume that he was *this* way or *that* way at any given point in the day. It was like those Nazi concentration camp guards who could come home from a day manning the gas chambers and be able to play games with their children, put a Bach record on the turntable, and make love to their wives before getting up to kill more innocents. And this was not the exception—this was the rule. The cousin of brutality is a terrifying normalcy. So I tried never to see these men in terms of black or white. I saw them instead in degrees of *soft* and *hard*. It was the soft that I was trying to locate inside them; once I could get my fingers into it, the advantage was mine. If sitting down with abhorrent people and treating them as friends is what it took to get through to that soft place, then I was more than happy to pour the Scotch.

There is a letter from the American president Abraham Lincoln that helps illustrate what I believed I was doing. Though he is remembered as the man who freed the slaves, his real objective in the civil war was keeping the United States together. And so he wrote to a friend: "If I could preserve the Union and not free any slave, I would do it. If I could preserve the Union by freeing all of the slaves, I would do it. If I could preserve the Union by freeing some slaves, and keeping others in bondage, I would do it." My only goal was saving the lives of the people upstairs, and questions of my taste in friendship were secondary—if they were relevant at all. If you stay friendly with monsters you can find cracks in their armor to exploit. Shut them out and they can kill you without a second thought. I reminded myself of this over and over.

Another principle helped me in these conversations, and it is this: Facts are almost irrelevant to most people. We make decisions based on emotion and then justify them later with whatever facts we can scrounge up in our defense.

When we shop for a car we make sure to investigate the gas mileage, look at the leg room, peer at the engine, and evaluate the cost, but the decision to buy it always comes down to a feeling in the gut. How will I look behind the wheel? Will it be fun to drive? What will my friends think? We congratulate ourselves later for a shrewd acquisition based on reasons a, b, and c, but the actual decision cannot be put in terms of an equation. People are really never as reasonable as they seem to be—in fact, "reason" is usually an afterthought, nothing more than a cover story for the feelings inside.

The same is true in politics. Let me give you a rather pertinent example. I seriously doubt the leadership of Rwanda really *believed* that average Tutsis were spies who had melted into the general population. I think they whipped up the flames of fear to create that belief. They were appealing to a dark place in the heart—that unreconstructed part of us that comes down from our ancestors, who lived in constant fear of beasts in the night. There was an emotional reason for people to hate and fear the Tutsi, and that nonsense about traitors in the villages was a set of "facts" grafted into place to justify the violence. And as I have said, the ethnic violence was only a tool for a set of cynical men to hold on to their power—which is perhaps man's ultimate emotional craving.

It is a dismal principle. But I could use it to save lives.

When I took that colonel into my office, poured him some beer, and puffed up his ego it was not about the facts of the matter at all. It was about his insecurity in his position and his need to feel like an important person. I created a web of words in which the choice I did not want to see him make—killing Thomas—was running counter to his emotional needs. I made him believe that such a loutish task was beneath him. And he bought it, even though he probably had the power to snap his fingers and have me and other troublemakers chopped to bits within twenty minutes. It is not that the colonel was a stupid man. Even the best of us can be slaves to our self-regard.

They kept coming and coming. From houses in Kabeza to besieged churches in Nyamirambo, they heard on the *radio trottoir* about the safe haven at the Mille Collines.

One of them was a man named Augustin Hategeka, who had run from his home with his pregnant wife when the killings broke out. They had taken refuge in a patch of forest and ate scavenged food for several days. Augustin had stood guard, watching for killers as she gave birth to their new son in the shade of a bush. Not knowing if he would live, they named him on the spot: *Audace,* French for "brave." With the help of some Hutu friends, the family found temporary refuge in St. Paul's pastoral center and I sent Army soldiers to fetch them to the Mille Collines. I met them at the entrance and made sure the baby was washed in hot water and covered in clean sheets.

I had known Augustin before the killings broke out and over the next several days we talked to each other about the things we had witnessed. Our conversation went something like this:

"My neighbors started killing my neighbors," he told me. "I saw people I have known for years taking out machetes and screaming orders. Old people were murdered. Children were murdered. I heard screams."

"I know," I told him. "The same thing happened in Kabeza."

"They chopped innocent people to pieces in the street. They cut the tendons in their legs so they could not run away."

"It is disgusting."

"I thought I knew these neighbors of mine," he told me.

"I don't think anybody knows anybody anymore," I told him.

We looked at one another across my desk. I knew what each of us was thinking: *Could we even trust each other?* I know for my part that I trusted nobody completely anymore. To relax my suspicions could mean death for me and everybody I was trying to protect. I had heard too many horrid stories by that point. Rwanda had gone insane.

I remember another guest, whom I will here call Jane, who had worked as a nurse alongside my wife. Her story was not out of the ordinary for Rwanda that spring. She had been married to a man named Richard, a stout man with eyeglasses who worked as a civil servant. He was a quiet man, one of those people you don't really notice in a group. That anyone would have considered those people a threat was ludicrous, Jane was of mixed race and the family had been marked for elimination. They tried to lie low in their house. A squad of *Interahamwe* broke inside and began to do their work. Jane managed to scramble into the kitchen and hide underneath a few sacks of charcoal. She stayed there while her husband and two children were cut into pieces in the other room. How she managed to remain quiet I will never know. She stayed under the coal for several hours and then crawled out to see the bodies of her family strewn about the front room. She fled from the house and, with the help of a neighbor, found her way to St. Paul's Church. We sent a car with policemen to pick her up. Her eyes were completely empty; it seemed the life had been washed out of them forever. I recognized the look. It was all over the hotel.

In all of this, I was fortunate to have a handful of soldiers who wore the blue helmet of the United Nations. I have previously expressed my disgust with the UN as a collective body, but those individuals serving in its name were capable of bravery. The men in my hotel displayed courage in going out onto the streets of Kigali to fetch the condemned. They were chauffeurs through hell. One in particular, a captain from Senegal named Mbaye Daigne, became legendary for his ability to dodge the *Interahamwe*. His companion, Captain Senyo of Ghana, displayed equal bravery at plucking refugees from their houses. It was a task that probably violated the ridiculous mission parameters handed down from New York, but these rules deserved to be broken.

These soldiers never used the hotel van; that would have been inviting death, because everybody in town knew that we were a haven for refugees. They used instead a white jeep with the UN logo. Rwandan soldiers also helped rescue people. One day they went out to find a prominent politician who had been hiding in a private house. On the way to the hotel they were stopped at a roadblock manned by an especially savage bunch of militia. There were corpses stacked up on either side, the hacked-up remains of people who had produced the wrong kind of identity card. The car got an unusually thorough search and they discovered the refugee hiding in the back.

"Where are you bringing this cockroach?" they demanded.

The soldier thought quickly. "We are taking him to the ministry of defense," he said. "Now let us pass before the Army starts to wonder where we are."

That was good enough for the militia and our refugee made it inside the Mille Collines without further incident. I suppose it was fortunate for us there were no cell phones in Rwanda in 1994, before the widespread use of cell phones. As we have seen, the violence was inherently full of chaos and mistakes. The chain of command was often vague and the orders were sometimes confusing. In such an environment it was therefore possible to make a convincing bluff that you were working for somebody in authority without anyone able to check your story. If there had been cell phones I think many who escaped death would have been killed instead. But that is not to say that the phones would have all worked for evil. I have said before that tools of murder can be turned into tools of life. If we had had cell phones in Rwanda, the *Interahamwe* would have been more efficient, but we also would have been able to coordinate more rescues right under their noses.

I used my secret fax phone many times to get a bead on where a given refugee might be hiding. One of them was my friend Odette Nyiramilimo, and her husband, Jean-Baptiste Gasasira, and their children, who I hoped was still in her house. In the first days of the genocide they had traded their family car, their stereo, their television, and other goods to some policemen in exchange for a ride south of Kigali, to where they thought they might be safe. But the policemen reneged, leaving my friends to try and flee through the marshes on their own. They were captured by *Interahamwe* and led in for interrogation, which they managed to escape. But in the chaos of war somebody made a mistake and put their names on the list of people who had been eliminated. Odette and Jean-Baptiste heard their own names being read on the rebel army's radio station as among those who had been killed. This took the heat away temporarily and, not knowing where else to go, they went back to their house and stayed out of sight, afraid even to answer the telephone. I rang and rang again. But one day when their food was almost gone, the phone started ringing.

"Don't pick it up!" ordered Jean-Baptiste.

"It's all the same," said Odette. "We are going to die of hunger here anyway." She answered the phone and it was me on the other end.

She could not have been more surprised. "We thought you were dead!" she said.

"I thought you were dead, too," I answered. "But don't go anywhere. I'm going to organize a rescue."

"Who are you going to send?"

"Froduald Karamira."

I meant it as a small joke, for he was a businessman who was notorious for his role in the massacres, but Odette missed my humor. "No, he will kill us all!" she said, and I made up a proverb on the spot: "If you want your goods to be safe, give them to a thief." Though she was in tears, she laughed. It was good to hear.

I negotiated again with Commander Habyarimana for the services of a Lieutenant named Nzaramba. His uniform and vehicle would give him partial, but not total, protection against the militias, and so it was going to be a risky operation. Not wanting to risk having the whole family in his jeep, Nzaramba made three separate trips. Odette came first with her son Patrick, and they were stopped at a roadblock close to the hotel.

"Where are you going?" they demanded.

She pulled out a supply of malaria pills and showed them to her would-be killer.

"I am coming to take care of the manager's children inside the Mille Collines," she said. "They are sick."

It worked. When she came in her eyes were glassy and far-away. I had not seen her since the killing had started.

"Odette, what may I bring you?" I asked her and could not have been more surprised to hear her say, "A beer." I had never seen her drink beer before. It went down in three gulps.

Once she came out of her daze Odette told me that being inside the Mille Collines was like being in a land of the resurrected dead; she was seeing many people who she had heard had been killed.

The next time Nzaramba went out he came back with Odette's children in the back of his jeep, and they too were stopped at a roadblock. This one happened to be right in front of the warehouse of an old friend of mine named Georges Rutaganda.

"Where are you going?" asked the man who leaned in their window. "Where are your parents?"

"My father is manning a roadblock and my mother is at the hospital," said Odette's son. The killers did not buy the story and withdrew to discuss what should be done. The machetes were just coming out when a car pulled up. Inside was Georges Rutaganda.

Let me pause here a minute and tell you about this man. We grew up together. He took an investment from his father and made quite a lot of money as the executive distributor of Carlsberg and Tuborg beer in Rwanda. He also went on to become the vice president of the *Interahamwe* and a man very close to the party of President Juvenal Habyarimana. I tried not to let this get in the way of our friendship. I did tell him several times before the killing started, "Listen, Georges. What you are doing is wrong. You are going down the wrong path." But he never got angry with me for my opinions. This absence of acrimony was a key element of our relationship. We both knew where the other stood politically. We had to stop visiting each other's families in the evenings, but our professional dealings continued, as did the presence of good feelings. It was like that German expression I mentioned earlier: *Dienst ist dienst und schnapps ist schnapps.* We continued to do business together even during the genocide. In fact, he was the main supplier of beer, toilet paper, and other necessities to the Mille Collines. Yet another irony of Rwanda: The man near the heart of the militia movement was making cash on the side by helping the refugees. I used these deal-making sessions to take him into my office and speak to him, as only one friend from the hills can do to another. "Listen, Georges," I would tell him, "I would like you to be very careful with my hotel. It would be very bad for me if any of your *Interahamwe* came inside. Please do me a favor and tell them it is off-limits."

Several people have criticized me for staying close to such a bad man, but I have never apologized for it. People are never completely good or completely evil. And in order to fight evil you sometimes have to keep evil people in your orbit. Even the worst among them have their soft side, and if you can find and play with that part of them, you can accomplish a great deal of good. In an era of extremism you can never afford to be an extremist yourself.

So at the roadblock Georges looked inside the car and saw children he thought he recognized.

"Aren't you the kids of Jean-Baptiste Gasasira?" he asked, and they nodded, frightened, not knowing what else to say. Now it was clear: They were cockroaches. They would be killed without further delay.

Georges then stepped in. Perhaps he had a soft spot for Odette and Jean-Baptiste, who had gone to the same university as he had in the 1970s. Perhaps he recalled that Jean-Baptiste had been his parents' personal physician. Perhaps this bankroller of the militias never agreed with the genocide that unfolded from his actions. I cannot say. But he turned to the captain of the roadblock and berated him.

"Let them go right now," he demanded. And one of the top officials of the murderous *Interahamwe* waved the lieutenant and the jeep and the children on toward the Mille Collines.

Just as I dealt with some questionable people during the genocide, I also sheltered some questionable guests. Several times in those days I drank cognac with a man named Father Wenceslas Munyegeshaka, who was the priest at the Sainte Famille church just down the hill from my hotel. He had abandoned the black robes of a priest and was wearing jeans and a T-shirt and carrying a pistol in his belt.

His church had been turned into a refuge for Tutsis, but the militias felt a lot more comfortable going inside it than they did the Mille Collines. Hundreds of people were taken from their refuge inside its redbrick walls and murdered elsewhere. And Father Wenceslas showed no interest in stopping it from happening. I knew that he even had a working telephone in the sacristy and I don't think he made phone calls to save anybody from execution, even though he also had political contacts.

One day when he was over having a drink my wife asked him, "Father, why don't you put on your robes and pick up a Bible instead of wearing a pistol? A man of God should not be wearing a pistol." For some reason, he directed his answer to me and not Tatiana.

"Listen, Paul," he said. "There have been fifty-nine priests become the sixtieth."

"If somebody comes and wants to shoot you," I said, "do you think that the pistol will protect you?"

It turned out that he had more reasons to be afraid than just his job. One day he came to the hotel with an elderly woman in tow. "Paul," he said, "I am bringing you my cockroach."

It was his own mother, a Tutsi. I assigned her to live in Room 237 without saying anything further.

Another person who found his way to us was a man I will call Fred, though that is not his real name. He was one of my neighbors from Kabeza, but not a very popular person. He had beaten an old man to death several years before and had been released from prison just before the genocide. He was a Tutsi, which made him an automatic target, but he was also a wanted man because he had three sons serving in the RPF. In the opening days of the genocide he was one of the neighbors who took shelter in my house. On that day, April 9, when the Army had come to take me to the Diplomates, he made several desperate comments, shaking as he spoke. "I know these people are looking for me. Let me go out there so they can kill me before they kill everyone here." Fred was not my best friend, but when he showed up later at the Mille Collines I was happy to see him alive and made sure that he got a place in a room and was protected from harassment by those who knew his story. There is no sin so great that somebody should die for it. When you start thinking like that you become an animal yourself.

I suppose Fred was another one of those wounded lions that my father had been so fond of talking about. There was a whole pack of them living in my hotel. By the end of May we had 1,268 people crammed into space that had been designed for 300 at most. There were up to 40 people living inside my own room. They were in the corridors, in the ballroom, on bathroom floors, and inside pantries. I had never planned for it to get this big. But I had made a promise to myself at some point that I would never turn anybody away. Nobody was killed. Nobody was wounded or beaten in the Mille Collines. That was an extraordinary piece of luck for us, but I do not think there is anything extraordinary about what I did for them with a cooler of beer, a leather binder, and a hidden telephone. I was doing the job that I had been entrusted to do by the Sabena Corporation—that was my greatest and only pride in the matter.

I am a hotel manager.

EIGHT

WAKING UP BEFORE THE SUNRISE has been my habit ever since I was a boy. I seem biologically incapable of sleeping in. Before the killing started that predawn quiet was one of my favorite times of the day. I would slip out of bed gently, so as not to wake Tatiana, and go out into the yard and putter around at various tasks. There was a radio on the outside ledge and I would listen to the news. I suppose it is that bred-in-the-bone Rwandan love for news. Besides, a hotel manager needs to know the gossip. This was one of the only times in the day I would have all to myself.

During the genocide I yearned to have one of those quiet mornings in the yard, when the news was just soccer scores and road closings instead of incitements to murder and lists of the dead. I still woke up in the hour before dawn, in a room jammed with people, and I craved that time when I was all alone. So I developed an early-morning ritual of visiting my favorite spot in the whole hotel.

To get there you take the stairs to the top floor. The rooftop restaurant and the conference rooms are down the hall to the right. You turn left off the staircase and enter the second unmarked door on the south side of the hallway. Behind this is another door, but this one is locked. You open it with a key that only the manager and the chief of security possess. You go up another flight of metal stairs, and there you are on the roof, with the whole of the city of Kigali spread out before you.

The hotel was built on the slope of Kiyovu Hill and the panorama is gorgeous. Even in the midst of war and death this aerie of mine had a peaceful aspect if you didn't look at any spot too closely and focused just on the hills and the sky. To look at the streets for longer than a few seconds was to see homes with broken windows, wrecked vehicles, roadblocks, and corpses everywhere. Better to focus on the distance than the details.

To the west, along the line of the far mountain ridge, you could see the road that snaked away down the valley. It led eventually to the city of Gitarama, where the crisis government held its seat. To the north was the area held by the rebel army. In the middle was Amahoro Stadium, where I knew there were over ten thousand refugees crammed inside, sleeping on the soccer field. It was a larger version of the Mille Collines, only with a different ethnic majority and living conditions that were far worse than what we had. There was nothing to cover anybody from the rain. Those who were wounded had no real medical care and their cuts grew infected and gangrenous.

There was nowhere for people to relieve themselves and so the field became a stinking heath.

Between the army lines was the no-man's-land. There is a saying in Rwanda: "The elephants fight, but it is the grass that suffers." Caught between the armies, we were the grass. When I came here at night I could see the flashes of gunfire and the red tracer bullets whizzing across the sky. But early mornings were calmer, the mortar shelling quiet and the popping of gunfire only occasional, heralding not a clash between troops but the killing of a lone victim or his family.

These mornings on my roof, with the sky melting to blue from purple, I took the time to prepare myself for what I knew was coming. I was going to die. I had done far too much to cross the architects of the genocide. The only question would be the exact time, and the method of my death, and that of my wife and our children.

I dreaded machetes. The *Interahamwe* were known to be extremely cruel with the people they chopped apart; first cutting tendons so the victims could not run away, then removing limbs so that a person could see their body coming apart slowly. Family members were often forced to watch, knowing they were next. Their wives and their children were often raped in front of them while this was happening. Priests helped kill their congregations. In some cases, the congregations helped kill their priests. Tutsi wives went to sleep next to their Hutu husbands and awoke to find the blade of a machete sawing into their neck, and above them, the grimacing face of the man who had sworn to love and cherish them for life. And Tutsi wives also killed their husbands. Children threw their grandparents down pit toilets and heaved rocks on top of them until the cries stopped. Unborn babies were sliced from their mothers' wombs and tossed about like soccer balls. Severed heads and genitals were on display. The dark lust unleashed in Rwanda went beyond friendships and beyond politics and beyond even hate itself—it had become killing for killing's sake, killing for sport, killing for nothing. It raged on, all around the hotel, on the capital's streets and in the communes and in the hills and in every little spidery valley.

There was a stash of money in the hotel safe. The money was for a last bribe, something to pay the militia to let me and my family be shot rather than face a machete.

Seven time zones away, in the United States, the diplomatic establishment was tying itself up in knots. Everybody wanted to avoid saying a certain word.

A Pentagon study paper dated May 1, 1994, sums up the prevailing attitude. The author was suggesting a way for the United States to take limited action in Rwanda without getting in too deep. "Genocide investigation: Language that calls for an international investigation of human rights abuses and possible violations of the genocide convention—*Be Careful.*

Legal at State was worried about this yesterday—Genocide finding could commit [the U.S. government] to actually 'do something.'" So the pressure was on. There had to be a way to call what was happening by something other than its rightful name.

It is not as though there was an information blackout. The U.S. government—and, in fact, most of its citizens who watched the news—knew what was taking place in Rwanda. Romeo Dallaire had made himself available to anyone who wanted to interview him by telephone, and had taken to calling the slaughter "ethnic cleansing." The BBC's courageous reporter Mark Doyle was granted access to the hopeless UN mission and filed a story every day about the ongoing slaughter. Journalists slowly realized this was more than just another African civil war. And by the end of May the broadcasts of the nightly television news and the newspapers in America were full of accounts of mass murders and bodies floating down Akagera River toward Lake Victoria. But even with this incontrovertible evidence the U.S. government would not let itself admit that what was happening was a genocide. This played right into the official lies of the *génocidaires:* The killings were a spontaneous uprising of grief among the villagers at the assassination of the president and not something that had been carefully planned.

The official U.S. State Department phrasing was nothing less than bizarre: "Acts of genocide may have occurred." When spokeswoman Christine Shelley was asked how many acts of genocide it takes to equal a genocide she did a clumsy dance by saying that it could not be determined if the violence was directed toward a certain ethnic group—never mind that five minutes of listening to RTLM would have told them all they needed to know. "The intentions, the precise intentions, and whether or not these are just directed episodically or with the intention of actually eliminating groups in whole or in part, this is a more complicated issue to address," she said. "I'm not able to look at all of those criteria at this moment and say yes, no. It's something that requires very careful study before we can make a final determination."

All in all, I would call this a very good *Rwandan no*.

The peculiar avoidance of the word *genocide* was for a reason. The word is actually a relatively new one in the English language. It was coined by a Polish-born lawyer named Raphael Lemkin who then helped persuade the United Nations to pass a resolution, in 1948, expressly forbidding the destruction of a group of people because of their religion, nationality, or ethnicity. Lemkin had been horrified by the Turkish slaughter of the Armenians during World War I, but was even more appalled that it seemed to be no crime in the conventional sense. Nations could not be held accountable for murder in the same way people could. Furthermore, there was nothing legal or otherwise that separated the random killing of civilians from the attempt to eliminate an entire race.

Grappling for a way to express the magnitude of the Nazis' plans for and actions against the Jews during World War II, Lemkin decided that we needed a new word to embody the concept. It had to be short and easy to pronounce and convey a certain horror. After some experimentation he chose *genocide*, blending the Greek word for "race" (*genus*) with the Latin word for "kill" (*cide*). The word caught on and was quickly added to *Webster's New International Dictionary*. UN member states signed a treaty in 1948 threatening criminal penalties for the leaders of any regime found to have conducted an extermination campaign against a particular religious or racial group. But the United States dragged its feet, fearing the encroachment of a world government telling it how to act. It was not until 1986 that the U.S. Senate finally ratified the agreement. By then genocides had been carried out in Cambodia, in Nigeria, in Pakistan, in Burundi, and in many other places on the globe.

But this is characteristic. As Harvard University scholar Samantha Power has pointed out, the world's foremost superpower, America, has almost never acted to stop a race of people from being exterminated, even when confronted with overwhelming evidence.

Lemkin's idea was romantic and idealistic: That it is in the interests of the entire interconnected human family to see that no one part of it is wiped out. And yet ever since, the short-term interests of national sovereignty have always carried the day. So it was with Rwanda, where "acts of genocide may have occurred" but no actual genocide that anyone really cared to see. If U.S. officials actually spoke the word out loud they might have been morally and legally compelled to act under the terms of the 1948 treaty. Few officials in Washington wanted that with a midterm congressional election around the corner. Everyone in the Clinton administration was mindful of the disaster in Somalia that had occurred the previous October, when eighteen Army Rangers were killed in the *Black Hawk Down* incident that seemed to symbolize everything that could go wrong with peacekeeping missions. Even though our situation was radically different in origin and nature, anything that called for a commitment of American troops to Africa was anathema in the halls of the U.S. State Department. And, of course, there was no natural resource in Rwanda that anybody cared about either—only human beings in danger.

I still wonder how policy officials from that time can sit down at the table with their families and have any appetite for food, or go to sleep at night, knowing that they failed to act. Human beings were sacrificed for political convenience. This would be enough, I think, to turn any reasonable man into a prisoner of his own conscience for the rest of his life.

Even a proposal to jam the frequencies of RTLM was rejected, on the grounds that the Army National Guard airplane required for the overflights cost eighty-five hundred dollars an hour to fly. If that plane had been kept aloft for every second of the genocide it would have worked out to about twenty-four dollars for each life taken that might otherwise have been saved.

Before the killing in the hotel could start they would have to get rid of me. I was standing between them and the prize targets inside. We had senators, doctors, ministers, priests, maids, peasants, housewives, intellectuals. Inside the Mille Collines was the remnant of what might be called the "Tutsi aristocracy"—the living embodiment of the phantom enemy that the hate radio was preaching against—as well as a good contingent of moderate Hutus who did not agree with the genocide. The hotel was becoming a holy grail of the killers, a giant resting place of cockroaches they were eager to wipe out for good. I was convinced we would be invaded by the militia any day. I knew also that that would mark the day of my death. We were all condemned prisoners, but we did not know the date of our execution, and we woke up every morning wondering if we were in our last few hours of consciousness.

In the early morning of April 23 I went to bed at around 4:00 A.M. I had spent several hours on the phone in the office, getting nowhere, as usual. I quietly unlocked the door of the suite so as not to wake up the other occupants, and fell into the spot that Tatiana had saved for me on the bed. I knew nothing but blackness for two hours and then I felt my wife pushing me. "There is someone on the phone that wants you," she said. You could still make phone calls at that point, and it was the reception desk asking for me.

A man whom I'll call Lieutenant Mageza came on the line. I knew him, but his voice sounded like cold marble. "Are you the manager?" he asked.

I was still fighting my way out of a deep sleep and my answer was thick.

"Yes. What is it?"

"I have an order from the Ministry of Defense for you to evacuate the hotel within thirty minutes," he said.

That woke me up.

"You want me to evacuate the hotel?"

"If you do not I will do it for you."

"What do you want me to tell the guests? Where are they going to go? Who is taking them? What security has been organized?"

The lieutenant was having none of it. "Do you not understand what I am saying? This hotel must be evacuated within thirty minutes. Tell the people here to 'go as they came.'" He used an expression in Kinyarwanda that means, in effect, if they came by car, they will leave by car. If they came on foot, they will leave by foot. The vehicles that had brought most of the guests were long gone, of course, and so most would have to simply walk away. This spelled certain death for nearly everybody in the hotel. But I didn't get the impression that the lieutenant was concerned.

I made an instant guess while I sat there in my underwear. If I was wrong, more than a thousand people would die. But I couldn't dwell on it; I had to take action. And my suspicion was that this lieutenant had not been ordered to do the killing himself. The idea was to shoo us out and let the street militia do the actual murdering. It would be less systematic, and many would surely get away, but it would eliminate the government's long-standing problem of the Mille Collines.

I decided then to—as the American phrase goes—kiss his ass.

"Yes, I understand what you are saying right now. I appreciate you informing me of the situation. I will comply with what you say. But can I please just have half an hour to get myself awake and get showered before I do what you want? Then I will begin the evacuation."

"Thirty minutes," he said, and hung up.

I did not wash. I did not even put my pants on. I ran five flights up to the roof and looked down at the street. What I saw opened a hole in my stomach. The militia had the place completely surrounded. There were hundreds of them holding spears, machetes, and rifles. It would be a killing zone here in an hour.

I raced down the stairs and back into my room, where I quickly calculated global time. It was early to be calling Europe, but far too late to be calling the United States, which had been worthless anyway. There was only one thing I could think to do: Get on the phone with somebody in the Rwandan Army who outranked the lieutenant and could order him to rescind his evacuation order. I pulled out the black binder and started calling all my generals. Though it was early in the morning I was able to reach several, and I described the threat with what I hoped was the right amount of urgency. Those that I reached knew that the Mille Collines was being set up and were not willing to say who had given the order. I was still phoning for help when a knock came at the door from a reception clerk. Somebody wanted to see me out front, he said. I started to dress, thinking it was probably the last time I would ever put on a pair of pants or button a shirt. Why hadn't I taken more pleasure out of these mundane tasks of everyday life?

I went down to the reception area to meet Lieutenant Mageza. I was surprised instead to see a very short man wearing the insignia of a colonel on his shoulder and assorted colorful medals on his chest. I recognized him as a high-ranking police officer named Ntiwiragabo.

"What is the situation here?" he asked.

"I have been asked to evacuate the hotel," I told him.

"The plan has been changed and this is why I'm here," he said.

I knew then that one of my phone calls had worked. This colonel had been sent over to help me. I told him that the order had been given by a lieutenant and that it was a very bad order that could have terrible repercussions for the Rwandan government. There would be killing outside that would shock the conscience of the world community.

The short colonel nodded, with an unfocused look in his eyes, and said that he would take care of the situation. I found out later that he had been sent over by the chief of the police, General Ndindiliyimana. His rank carried the day. The militia and the soldiers were immediately dispersed and the evacuation order was called off. The lieutenant, who I later learned was the nephew of a top *génocidaire,* had stolen away.

I thanked the colonel profusely.

"Sir, you have saved lives today," I told him.

"I am only doing my job," he told me curtly, and walked away.

I knew this peace was fragile, and so I decided to switch from ass kissing to bluster. What I was about to try was a serious risk, but I saw it as the only way to insure that an invasion could be prevented for at least the next few days. I paced around for a few minutes, took a deep breath, and then telephoned the Diplomates Hotel and asked for Colonel Théoneste Bagosora, one of the leaders of the genocide, who was staying in Room 205.

"Colonel," I said in my most officious voice, "I am sorry to disturb you. I have received an order from the Ministry of Defense to close down the Mille Collines, and as the general manager of all Sabena properties in Rwanda, I must therefore also close the Diplomates."

I could practically hear his veins bulging on the other end of the phone.

"*Who* has given such orders?!" he screamed at me.

"I do not know; they were relayed through a lieutenant. He said his name was Mageza."

"If you try to close this hotel, we will break down the doors to get back inside."

"If you want, you can do that, but it is my duty and obligation to close down all the Sabena hotels in Rwanda," I told him. "I didn't want to take you by surprise. I only want you to have enough time to pack your things."

He was silent for a minute.

"Well, that order has now changed."

This is what I was waiting to hear. But I decided to press my advantage even further. Sometimes, when you have a man temporarily on the ropes, it is better to secure all the concessions you can. I tried to forget I was talking to a man who could have squashed me like a bug. We had known each other slightly before the genocide, but we had little in common, and there was no pretense of either of us doing any favors. I think he must have been afraid of the French. I felt very much like a small boy whacking a vicious dog with a stick—and getting away with it.

"Colonel, we can come to a compromise," I told him, as if *I* was the one who had the power to dictate terms. "I will not close the Diplomates. But I need water over here. Can you please send us back the water truck you took away from the Mille Collines?"

"Yes, yes," he said impatiently.

"There is another thing," I told him. "There are a group of people staying in the manager's house of the Diplomates. They are valuable employees. We need them over here. Can you please see that they arrive at the Mille Collines safely?"

I think this was the first he knew that there even *was* a manager's cottage, let alone that a group of my neighbors had been staying there this whole time, right under the noses of the *génocidaires*. They had been kept fed by a courageous bellboy.

Bagosora didn't waste any more time. "Yes, fine, good-bye," he said, and hung up.

Within the hour a red Toyota pickup pulled up to the Mille Collines. Inside were the neighbors I had not seen since the day their lives were purchased with francs from the hotel safe. A truck also arrived to refill our swimming pool and we had fresh water to drink for the first time in weeks. It was courtesy of one of the vilest proponents of genocide that Central Africa has ever seen. Somewhere I could hear my father laughing.

NINE

ONE OF THE MOST HONEST CONVERSATIONS I had during the genocide happened near the end of it.

General Augustin Bizimungu, the Army chief of staff, came to see me in my room. It was one of the few times in those few months that I didn't need anything from him. Neither did he want anything from me. And we drank and talked for several hours.

He looked awful. There were folds of darkened skin hanging under his eyes. He seemed to have aged twenty years since the time before the killing started. We talked about the rebel army advancing from the east. They had been making slow but steady progress toward Kigali aiming to link up with their detachment dug in at the parliament building. RPF leader Paul Kagame had fewer troops but while in exile he had instilled an impressive level of discipline and commitment into his army. Not for nothing was the international press calling him "the Napoleon of Africa."

There was now some talk of a swap between the warring

armies: The rebels would release the Hutu refugees in Amahoro Stadium if the Rwandan Army would let the people inside the hotel go over to the rebel side. These discussions filled me with hope, but they also terrified me. Getting free from the constant threat of slaughter seemed like a kind of heaven, but to label the hotel as a rebel prize seemed incredibly dangerous. I was afraid it would only boost our attractiveness as a target for the doped-up militias, who were a law unto themselves and followed the orders of the Army only when they felt like it. Bizimungu slumped in his chair as we talked, his drink barely touched beside him.

"Listen, general," I finally said. "You are now the leader of a bunch of killers and looters and rapists. Are you sure you can win?"

His reply astonished me.

"Paul, I am a soldier," he said. "We lost this war a long time ago."

Perhaps he had an inkling of what would be in store for him: a human rights tribunal and lifetime imprisonment in a jail cell. Or perhaps he had grown tired of all the murders around him. I am not certain what he was thinking then, but I saw that he could no longer hide the aura of defeat around him and his soldiers. I also knew that we were drawing near to the end of the war.

The restoration of a sane world was something I had dreamed about. I would likely die in the transition from chaos back to order, but at least it would all be over.

On May 3, the United Nations attempted to evacuate the Hotel Mille Collines.

The Army and the rebels had struck a deal: A few dozen refugees from the stadium would be swapped for an equal number of refugees from the hotel. They would be taken to the airport and whisked out of the country.

There was a terrible catch for us, though. Only those refugees who could secure invitations from people living abroad would be allowed to leave the hotel. This seemed very unfair to me. As a practical matter those people most likely to have overseas contacts were the rich and the powerful. The Tutsi and moderate Hutu peasants we had with us had virtually no chance of leaving. But these were the conditions that had been negotiated by the armies and I was in no position to argue. This rule, I think, came from the African love of bureaucracy and process. Even in the best of times there were many senseless permissions that had to be acquired to get anything done, and this culture of paperwork did not change even during the genocide. By that point, however, my friends and I had become specialists in the art of forgery, and we created fake letters for a number of those who had no overseas friends.

This put me in an awkward position, for I happened to be one of those privileged few who could legitimately arrange for transport out of the country for me and my family. *Out.* There seemed to be no more seductive concept: out of this phantasmagoria of knives and blood, out of the dark rooms that smelled like feces and sweat, out of this entire pointless conflict and the idiotic life-or-death ethnic definitions and away from the power-drunk fools with their empty smiles and machetes and into a safe place of clean sheets and air-conditioning and warm baths and no worry about anything at all that mattered. Out.

I could have it. I could have it *tomorrow.*

But I could not. I really could not. I knew that if I took this opportunity to leave I would be removing one of the only remaining barriers in between the militias and the guests. Nobody here would be left to present themselves—however flimsily—as a middleman standing in between the killers and the refugees. Nobody else had those years of favors and free drinks to cash in. I could donate my black binder to somebody else, but it would be useless to them. If I left and people were killed I would never be at peace. My food would never taste good again; I could never enjoy my freedom. It would be as though I had killed those people myself. The refugees had even come to me and said, "Listen, Paul. We are told you are leaving tomorrow. Please let us know so that we can go to the roof of the hotel and jump because we cannot bear to be tortured with machetes."

But one thing I did for myself: I used my contacts with the Sabena Corporation to secure invitations out for my whole family. I was not so courageous a man that I could bear to see my family in danger any longer. I sincerely hoped that I would not be depriving anybody more needy through this action, but it was what I felt was the best choice under terrible circumstances. If I saw my wife or children murdered when I *knew* I once had the chance to see them to safety my life would be ruined. This was the most painful decision I have ever made in my life. I had decided to stay and face whatever would come.

Beyond this I had no control over who would be staying or leaving. This was a profound relief, because I did not want to have that decision over life or possible death. On May 2, I, with the refugee committee, presented a list to the United Nations soldiers of all those refugees who had obtained invitations via my fax telephone. Handing over that list made me extremely uncomfortable. To begin with, the whole idea of lists now had an evil connotation in Rwanda. We suspected that by handing over such a list, we would be informing the militias who was leaving and who was staying. This could have put their lives in danger. But I had no choice but to deliver the required list. All I could do was hope that the UN would not let it leak to the killers.

Around midnight, I found my wife and children awake in our room. I previously had not had the courage to tell them I would not be going with them in the evacuation, but the time had arrived. I pretended my children were asleep and not listening and I told my wife, "I had made a different decision. I am remaining with the refugees. You are leaving."

Everyone then raised their voices and talked as if they were one person.

"What about you? You keep talking about us."

"Listen. I am the only person here who can negotiate with these killers outside."

"But how can you stay?"

"If people inside this hotel are killed, I will never be able to sleep again. I'll be a prisoner of my own conscience.

"Please," I told them. "Please accept and go."

The next day, at approximately 5:30 P.M., I saw my wife and children off at the roundabout in front of the hotel. They and the other fortunate guests were loaded into UN trucks while I watched from under the canopy near the door. I even helped them climb inside. I tried to be almost casual about it, telling them I would see them soon, as if they were off to the grocery store, but inside my heart was breaking. I said nothing special, nothing *climactic*, because that would have upset everybody, me most of all. I watched the first truck go by, and then the second. In Rwandan culture it is never acceptable for a man to cry, but I came very close that evening. I made it through those awful minutes the same way I made it through the entire genocide: by losing myself in the details of work.

I was then forty years old. Everything I had in life was pulling away in those trucks, and it was my decision to stay and face probable execution. I knew that I was taking all the responsibility now. That gave me a little peace.

Out in the front courtyard, many people had their transistor radios turned on RTLM, and I heard the names of my wife and children being read aloud, along with the other refugees who had just pulled away. "The cockroaches are escaping," said the announcer. "Stop all the cockroaches from leaving the Mille Collines. Put up roadblocks. Do your work. Do not leave the grave half full."

The list had leaked. Somebody from the hate radio had apparently stolen it or bought it from the United Nations or the Rwandan Army. I even saw a correspondent from RTLM standing in the parking lot.

There are no good words to describe what it is like to hear an execution order broadcast for your own family, and to know that you played a role in putting them in death's hands. Their beautiful names—Tatiana, Tresor, Roger, Lys, Diane— were a profanity in that announcer's mouth. I felt as if he was raping them with his voice. I hated him, hated RTLM, hated the genocidal power brokers, hated the stench of the hotel, hated the dank hallways, and hated the pride I once had in my country and my job. I hated that I was utterly powerless to save my family. I wanted to follow the jeeps in my own car, but the roadblocks would surely catch me alone and I would die like the other eight hundred thousand. All I could do was frantically work the phones.

When she was able to speak again Tatiana told me what happened.

The first convoy of sixty-three refugees was escorted by eight soldiers wearing the blue helmets of the UN. They were stopped at a roadblock two kilometers away from the hotel, at a place called Cyimicanga, where some men from the *Interahamwe* were standing alongside a few observers from the Rwandan Army. All the evacuees in the trucks were ordered out onto the roadside dirt. The street boys at the barricades had been given Kalashnikovs, and one of them fired an opening shot into the dirt near the feet of a refugee named Immaculate. It also happened to come perilously close to a soldier. A second shot struck and killed a member of the Presidential Guard.

"They are going to kill us!" somebody screamed, and that caused the militia to get even angrier. They used their rifle butts to start beating the refugees. Men were slugged in the gut, women were slapped across the face, children were kicked. A few used their machetes to cut open the skin on the forearms of some of the captives: It was the usual sick prelude to a total dismemberment. My wife was worked over particularly hard; she was thrown into a truck with a back so twisted she could barely move.

The UN soldiers, meanwhile, were disorganized. Some were bravely trying to insert themselves between the militia and their intended victims, but my wife told me the Bangladeshis put their hands in the air like stick-up victims. It would have been almost funny if it hadn't been such a signal for the militia to do as they pleased. This fiasco at the roadblock would have made a perfect metaphor for the ineptitude of the UN, but the last two months in Rwanda had created so many of those images that they hardly seemed worthy of note anymore.

My son Roger was approached by a boy he had known from school, a former classmate and friend. "Give me your shoes, you cockroach," said the boy.

Roger obeyed without protest and gave over his tennis shoes to his old friend, who was now a killer with a machete. They had once played soccer together. I suppose it was an echo of the meaningless gulf that had opened that day in 1973 between myself and my best friend, Gerard. My son was now experiencing much the same thing, only now he was the unlucky one.

Ah Rwanda, why?

The only thing that saved the caravan was the bitter argument between the Army and the militia. They were beginning to open fire on each other. Some of the UN soldiers saw their chance. They picked up the refugees in the dirt, threw them into the trucks like lumber, and roared off back toward the Mille Collines before the militia could regroup.

I ran out to the roundabout to meet them coming back and found my wife lying in a puddle of blood on the floor of one of the trucks. She was moaning slightly.

"Can you move?" I asked. She shook her head.

I was nearly blind with a red whirling of fury and relief and fright, but I had a job to do and I forced myself to stay in control. We took the wounded off the trucks and led them back into the hotel they had thought they were escaping. We called for Dr. Gasasira and another doctor named Josue, who began to bandage up the cuts imediately. The Mille Collines was full of people screaming and crying and hugging one another. I took Tatiana up to our room, 126, and made sure she was resting on the bed. Her eyes were blank with shock. The children were unhurt but completely quiet.

Once I was sure that our wounded were all being tended to, I rushed to my office. There was no time to spare. We needed more protection immediately. It was now clear that the government and the militias knew the identities of many of the high-profile refugees we were hiding. They might not chance an all-out invasion of the Mille Collines, but they might begin a series of individual assassinations. I was terrified that their bloodlust had been aroused beyond the point of control. I had already taken the precaution of finding an outdated guest list to give to any killer who might come asking for it at the reception desk. I had also ordered the room numbers pried off the doors to further confuse anyone who came in here looking for a specific target. But more protection was crucial. I called everyone I knew who was still alive. And then I called them again, insisting we have more policemen posted outside.

It seems strange to say, but it was a relief to be *doing* something, even if it seemed like I was getting nowhere. It was one big extended *Rwandan no* from all my military friends and, of course, the UN. Not until our last night in the hotel was I finally given five Tunisian soldiers from the UN contingent to safeguard the parking lot, and by then it was too late to make a difference.

We did not have long to rest. On the morning of May 13 at 10 A.M. I was visited in my office by a Rwandan Army intelligence agent named Lieutenant Iradakunda. I had known him only slightly, but my impression had been that he was a less than loyal supporter of the ongoing genocide. My suspicions were confirmed when he took me aside to a quiet area.

"Listen, Paul," he said. "We are going to attack you today at 4:00 P.M."

"Who?" I asked. "How many?"

"I do not know details."

"Are they coming to kill or are they coming to clear it out?"

"I do not know details. Don't ask me for a solution. But I am telling you this as a friend: 4:00 P.M." And with that he turned and left.

I had only a few hours. I went straight to my office and began calling names in my book, pleading with them to lobby the *Interahamwe* to call off the raid. If that was impossible, could I at least get some more protection from policemen or the military? It was clear that I would have to invoke some international pressure to stop the raid, and so I started pestering the White House, the Quai d'Orsay, the Belgian government—anybody I could think of.

One of the calls I made, of course, was to my bosses at Sabena, who shared my panic and pledged to raise hell with the French government. This "French connection" was a key pressure point that already saved us from disaster many times. I was going to press on it once more—hard. Let me explain.

The Hutu Power government maintained close ties to France throughout the genocide. It was the French who had provided military training and armaments to most of the Rwandan Army and smuggled French guns kept flowing in through neighboring countries even after Habyarimana's plane was shot down. Even the *Interahamwe* knew who their friends were. They were under strict instructions not to harm or harass any French nationals who came through their roadblocks. Belgians, meanwhile, were supposed to be murdered on sight. It was the height of idiocy to think that a lost tourist necessarily supports or even agrees with every tangled fine point of the foreign policies of their home nation, but that was what passed for logic in Rwanda during those times.

A general panic in the hotel would have been disastrous, so I told only a few refugees of the upcoming deadline. I dialed the world, with the clock ticking down. We had a few weapons in the hands of our policemen. We had some cash. Some drinks. But I didn't think it would be enough to bribe our way out of a wholesale raid. When four o'clock arrived I stood near the entrance and waited. And nothing happened. No mobs were gathered behind the bamboo fence. Perhaps the leadership was late in arriving. Or perhaps the lieutenant's information was off by an hour. Five o'clock ticked by. And then six. The sun went down and there was nothing but quiet. I did not relax. It seemed that one of my telephone pleas had gotten through—I could not be sure which one—but it may have only purchased a temporary stay.

At about 10:00 P.M., a rocket-propelled grenade smashed into the south wall just above the second floor. It tore a hole in a staircase wall and blew out the glass in Rooms 102, 104, and 106, but nobody was injured. I braced for an invasion, but that single shot was all that came. I immediately got on the secret phone with General Dallaire and told him we were being attacked. But no further rounds were fired. Dallaire showed up about half an hour later with a squad of subordinates and looked at the damage. They were joined by a Congolese soldier who had earned my lasting disrespect after I saw him try to buy a four-wheel-drive car from a refugee.

I can still see this group milling about the swimming pool deck, trying to decide where the missile had come from. One pointed to the headquarters of the gendarmerie down the valley. Another pointed off toward the RPF lines. They argued and gestured, apparently unable to make up their minds.

About half an hour later they left with a shrug. Would there be more rockets fired at us? There was no way to tell. There wasn't anything I could do to prevent it from happening; all I could do was try to keep my cool when and if it happened. Nearly delirious with fatigue after what had been one of the longest days of my life, I crawled into bed beside my wounded wife and fell into a dark unconsciousness.

To my huge surprise things became quiet for a few weeks after that. Once again my premonitions of my death were mistaken. We still saw the killers moving on the sidewalks behind the bamboo, but there were no invasions and no random violence. No more missiles were fired. We counted down the days until May 26, when the United Nations, the Army and the rebels wanted to make a second try at an evacuation. This time they would send us not to the airport but to a hill behind the rebel lines.

My friends made several attempts to convince me to sign up for it. No way, I said. There were hundreds of refugees who would not be evacuated and they still needed my protection, for the same reasons I had cited when I refused to go along with the first evacuation. And this time I would not allow Tatiana and the kids to go either. I did not trust the UN. My wife was now able to sit up in bed, and even walk around a bit, but she was shaken and frail and frightened of every bump in the hallway. I also felt that even if they got out safely it would be a sign to the *Interahamwe* that I trusted the rebels to take better care of my wife and children. That would be pushing things far too far. I had been skating on paper-thin ice for so long, but even my oldest friends in the highest ranks of the Army would not be able to stomach that sign of treachery. They would not be there to help when the militias came in. Their continuing friendship was my one lifeline, even though it was as thin as a sewing thread.

"But these thugs know you are the one who has been protecting everybody," said Odette. "They will surely kill you."

"I would never be able to face myself again if anybody dies," I told her. "And if my wife and my children go with you they will see that I have taken a side. They will not hesitate to come kill me."

The night before the evacuation four families gathered in Room 126. We were all old friends. In the room were: Odette and Jean-Baptiste and their four children; John Bosco Karangura and his three children; journalist Edward Mutsinzi and his wife and child; and Tatiana and me and our four children.

We were going to do a *pacte de sang*—a blood oath. It is one of the most powerful bonds you can form with someone in Rwanda. It is the same *igihango* game I played as a boy, except the stakes are higher and the friendship is not a secret one. You are supposed to cut yourself in the stomach along with your friend and drink the other person's blood from your hands. Few people took that physical step anymore, not since the advent of AIDS, but you could still make a verbal pledge. Other than the promise you made to marry somebody, it was the most solemn vow you could make.

"Listen to me," said Jean-Baptiste. "Listen to me all the children here. Look around. You see all the adults in here. We have decided from here onward to become brothers and sisters. If your parents should be killed, then the adults in the room tonight, then they become your parents. Get away from danger and find them if you can. Everyone in here has promised to raise the orphans as their own children. And if all the adults should be killed, then the oldest child will take care of everyone."

We did not cut our bellies and mix our blood, but we all sipped from a glass of red wine as a symbol of the promise we had made. We all stood up, many of us crying, and shook hands. There were bitter tears in the room that night, but also love. We had been through a sea of fire and we clung to one another, not knowing if we would ever see one another again or even be breathing after the next twelve hours. I am a hotel manager and I don't usually think in terms of such finalities, so

I can only say that when death is all around and life is draining away by the second, that is when humanity can be so sweet and so fine.

The evacuation started much like the first, with stony good-byes that did not match the emotion of the previous night. I watched my friends pull away and went back inside. This convoy was much better organized than the first, and the militias had been ordered to keep their distance. Several hundred were moved out that day, leaving the Mille Collines still jammed with people, but feeling oddly empty.

"Most of the traitors have gone to join the cockroaches," said the radio. But the threat never stopped. On June 17, early in the morning, the killings flared up at the Sainte Famille Church, which was barely half a kilometer away from us, just down the hill. It is one of Kigali's premier Catholic churches, and was a major site of refuge. There were at the entrance to the hotel dozens of people snatched inside its redbrick walls. The RPF had staged a daring rescue one night, leaving those left behind vulnerable to attack. From the roof I could see the crowds of militias circling like insects around a light. I was afraid the violence would inevitably spill over on the hotel. After two and a half months of nonstop slaughter this was the one place in Kigali where nobody had died. It was, for that reason, a kind of trophy.

During this particular crisis I finally blew my cool. It

happened when I was talking in the lobby with the mayor of Kigali, a man I had known for years. He was also a colonel in the Army and someone in a position to help us.

"The militia are killing people at Sainte Famille Church," I told him. "Surely they will also kill refugees here. I want soldiers with a lot of strength here to protect us."

"Paul, I tell you I cannot spare any more police to help you. It is not possible."

"Do you not understand the situation here? This is what has just happened. You can see it all from my roof if you want. The militia has attacked innocent civilians. It will happen again."

"There is nothing I can do."

"Listen, my friend" I said, feeling my anger welling up inside. Anybody who knows me will tell you that when I start to call a person "my friend" it usually means I am feeling the opposite.

"Listen to me now," I repeated. "One day all this will be over, and on that day you and I will have to face history. What will they say about us? Are you willing to say that you denied protection when it mattered and that innocent people died because of it? Are you sure this is the answer you want to give history?"

I don't know what made me choose those particular words. As a failed pastor I suppose I should have invoked God, as in, Listen, my friend, when we die we will have to give an account to heaven. But somehow it seemed more appropriate to remind him of history's indelible record.

I have told you that Rwandans have a special ear for their own history; we take it seriously in a way that few other nations do. It is what caused us to pick up arms against ourselves and kill each other. Perhaps this registered with my friend the mayor. In any case, he was offended by what I had said. He turned away without another word and stalked out of the Mille Collines. He left me standing alone and frightened. I worried that I had lost a key friend, and my friends were all that were keeping us alive.

That same day, at noon, I had an appointment to see General Bizimungu, who was at the Diplomates. It was one of the few times I ventured outside the grounds of the Mille Collines since I had arrived there nearly seventy days earlier. The trip was only five minutes long but it wound past the heaps of corpses and bloodstains on the road that seemed like natural parts of the scenery now. I met the general in the lobby and took him immediately down to the wine cellar, where I knew there would be some remaining stocks of Bordeaux and Côtes du Rhône or something else I could give him. It was now my habit. If I survived the genocide, I thought ruefully, it would be a long time before I could interact with anyone in a position of power without feeling the urge to stockpile a favor with him.

We talked about the war and he repeated the mournful prediction that he had made in my hotel room. The government was losing. They could hold the lines temporarily, but their supplies were running low. The rebels had too much momentum and superior military. They would be flooding into Kigali before long and would perhaps put all the leadership on trial for war crimes. But in the midst of all the murder and insanity, the government of Rwanda had continued to do business as if everything was functioning normally.

It occurred to me that this wine cellar had also been the scene of a strange conversation I had had with General Augustin Ndindiliyimana of the National Police force several weeks earlier. He was the one who had dismantled the road-block for me on April 12, and a man whose continued friendship was helping keep us alive. I had come down here with him to look for a drink and he took the opportunity to tell me something absurd. He had just been appointed our nation's ambassador to Germany.

"Are you going to go?" I asked him.

"If the RPF agrees," he said. This surprised me. He was speaking about the rebel army as if it was already the government of Rwanda.

Bizimungu shared this dim view of his own fortunes, and as we talked amid the dusty bottles of wine, I wondered how much longer he was going to be able to hang on.

Our surreal conversation was interrupted by the arrival of one of the general's staff who came with an urgent message: "The militia has entered the Mille Collines."

So this was it. My worst nightmare was coming true and I wasn't even there to see it happen. My children. My wife.

My friends. All those people.

"General, let's go back to the Mille Collines," and he did not hesitate to come with me. It seemed that he was just as eager to be there as I was. On that drive through downtown Kigali it came to me quite calmly that this was almost surely the end of my life, the last day I would ever exist. I regarded this probability without a great deal of interest. I had contemplated my own death so many times in the last two and a half months that it had lost whatever power it had once had to upset me. All I wanted to do anymore was the work in front of me; I had lost the desire for everything else. At some point in that strange twilight of the genocide I had taken leave of myself as a sentient person. My only existence anymore was in my actions. And when those actions were halted it would be no more remarkable than the mindless tug of gravity terminating the roll of a child's rubber ball. Death no longer frightened me.

But I still thought I might be of some use.

When we passed the roadblock near the front of the hotel I saw that nearly every one of the killers was gone—a very bad sign. The driver sped us to the front entrance. I heard General Bizimungu deliver an order to the sergeant with us. I'll never forget what he said:

"You go up there and tell those boys that if one person kills anyone I will kill them! If anybody beats anyone I will kill them! If they do not leave in five minutes I will kill *all* of them!"

I ran inside the hotel, feeling as though I were underwater, and discovered the reception desk unmanned. But I heard shouting and crashing upstairs. One of the *Interahamwe* was in the corridor. He was dressed in ragged clothes and holding onto a rifle. He stared at me. I was wearing a plain white T-shirt and black pants.

"Where is the manager?" he demanded of me.

"I think he went that way," I said, pointing down a corridor. And then I strode off in the opposite direction. I could always give that *Rwandan no* with the best of them.

Once I was out of his sight I slipped upstairs. The militia had broken down several room doors, to make sure they had discovered everyone. The door to 126 had also been smashed open. So they had found my family.

I went inside the room, wondering if I would see their corpses. But the room was untouched. There did not appear to be any signs of a struggle. I went inside the bathroom and something motivated me to peek behind the shower curtain. There they all were, clustered in the arms of my wife, staring back at me.

Relief flooded over me, but I had to see what was happening to the others. I told them to stay put without making a peep, dashed down the stairs, and ran down that spiral staircase near the bar and out to the back lawn, where I saw all my guests on their knees near the swimming pool. This quiet square of water had once been the shadow capital of Rwanda and now it appeared to be the site of an imminent massacre. The militia was strutting around, demanding that everybody put their hands in the air. One of the men waved his machete in the air. I saw one of my receptionists among the militia—I had always suspected him of being a spy.

They had herded everyone to the swimming pool. By that point I thought it was generally understood that everyone inside the Mille Collines was a refugee from the militia and thus had reason to be killed. Why the need for formalities? Why not just start the killing machine? The only thing I could imagine was that they were aiming to shove the dead bodies into the swimming pool to foul the water for any refugee who might have escaped their notice.

Whatever the reason, the delay saved us all.

I saw Bizimungu inside the hotel, chanting his angry command. He emerged onto the pool deck now, enraged, his khaki and camouflage well pressed, his pistol drawn, his face taut with anger. Bizimungu was known as a quiet man, almost timid by military standards, but I had seen him angry a few times before and his temper was volcanic. He roared out his order again: "If one person kills anyone I will kill them! If anybody beats anyone I will kill them! If you do not leave in five minutes I will kill *all* of you!"

There was a moment of surprise. The militiamen looked at one another, as if seeking the approval of the group for whatever actions would follow. The lives of hundreds hung in their uncertainty. They could easily have disobeyed him. Bizimungu was a powerful man with powerful allies, but there had been hundreds of mutinies against Army officers during the genocide—thousands of unapproved murders. And this was the Hotel Mille Collines: the citadel of Belgian arrogance, the luxurious island of privilege, the best redoubt of cockroaches anywhere in Rwanda. Didn't the general see what kind of prize he was giving up?

I saw surly looks on the faces of several of those boys. Their lust had been rising and now it had been denied. They were primed to kill and this traitor general had put a stop to it. I could tell they now wanted to turn their fury onto him. But they didn't. They lowered their machetes and began to file out.

General Augustin Bizimungu now sits in a jail cell. He will probably be there the rest of his life.

After the genocide he fled to Zaire, and then into far-away Angola. He was captured by local police there and brought before the International Criminal Tribunal that was organized to prosecute war crimes committed during the genocide of 1994. Bizimungu was charged with supervising the arming and training of the militias. As I write this, he has not yet been convicted. He is now held in Arusha, the same city in Tanzania that had hosted the ill-fated peace talks that led to the final outbreak of hostilities between the Rwandan Army and the rebels.

I have been criticized for my friendship with him during the genocide, but I have never apologized for it. "How could you have stayed close to such a vile man?" I am asked, and my answer is this: I do not excuse whatever he may have done to promote the genocide, but I never heard him agree with any of the bloodshed when he was in my presence. I had to stay close to him because he could help me save lives. I would have stayed close with anyone who could help me do that.

He is a man who cannot be judged in stark terms. Like almost all men, there are hard places and soft places inside and the final verdict can never be a simple one. There is a saying in Rwanda: "Every man has a secret corner of his mind that nobody will ever know." And I do not think I know enough about Bizimungu's secret corner to judge him. He may well have done terrible things in Rwanda before and during the genocide, but I know that he stepped in for me at crucial moments to save the lives of innocent people when it was of no conceivable benefit to him.

If I had ended that friendship, I do not think I would be here to write these words today. There are also at least 1,268 people who survived the killing partly because of the instructions of Bizimungu. In my book that counts for something.

The aborted slaughter at the Mille Collines was what it took to convince all parties that the hotel must be cleared out without further dithering. The United Nations, the rebels, and the Rwandan Army conferred and decided to do it that very day. They assigned us those five Tunisian soldiers to guard the parking lot for the last night. It made me furious that they were given to us long after we needed them, but there was no point in making a scene. On that afternoon I busied myself with making sure everybody was out of their rooms safely. There was a line of jeeps and trucks outside, the third such time that an evacuation convoy had been assembled there, but I had a feeling this would truly be the last one.

I made a last check of the hotel where I had spent seventy-six of the longest days of my life. Though I had been convinced I would die inside of it I felt affection for the place. When I was a young man it was where I had found my true occupation. I had met some of the most generous people in my life within its walls. Sabena gave me a job when I needed one and taught me things I never would have learned otherwise. They showed me how to respect myself by respecting others. When the killing started the hotel had saved people. It had projected the image of an ultimately sane world that kept the murderers at bay. I am not a particularly sentimental man, but I felt the odd urge to stroke it like a pet dog.

I made sure that the hotel was empty of everybody who wanted to go. Some employees had asked to stay, and I let them. I couldn't tell how many had been spies for the militia all along. By that point I was beyond caring. It was time to leave. When the UN convoy pulled away I was in the backseat of the last jeep. I hid under a plastic tarp for fear that the militias would recognize me and shoot at me as we drove by the roadblocks. The Mille Collines had been one of the very few places in Kigali where nobody was killed.

TEN

IN THE TIME BEFORE THE GENOCIDE it had been fashionable for the elite to buy country estates near a region named Kabuga just outside the capital. The area is attractive, with low hills and unusually large plantations full of grazing livestock. Almost everyone in Rwanda, no matter how long they have lived in a city, keeps close connections with the soil, and even a lifelong office worker probably has a few goats to call his own in a village somewhere outside the capital. The biggest gentlemen-farmer flocks, however, were at Kabuga. It was the best weekend address in the nation.

We were hustled there by the Rwandan Patriotic Front, which had turned it into a kind of refugee holding area. But it was no camp in the conventional sense. It was a looting zone.

Soldiers from the rebel army had stolen food from all the shops. Potatoes had been dug out of the fields. Goats had been captured and slaughtered. This made me furious. It was the same kind of impunity we had seen in 1959 during the Hutu Revolution, only this time it was yesterday's victims who were helping themselves to the spoils. War is hell, and ugly things happen in its midst—I know this. But they always create permanent resentments that have a way of erupting later in history. The casual disrespect for other people and their property was what helped create the genocide we had just lived through. I was afraid I was watching the conception of another. It made me feel as though Rwandans had learned nothing at all.

It therefore does not make me proud to tell you this: I, too, was among those who had to forage for food. I can only say that it was a choice between that or going hungry. My family and I also slept in the house of an unknown family who had fled the advancing rebel army. I can only hope these strangers would forgive us today. I never knew who they were, but it made me terribly uncomfortable to be using their property.

There was a surprise in the camp. We spotted the children of my wife's brother—the man who I had been dining with on the terrace of the Diplomates on the night Habyarimana's plane had been shot down. Anaise was two and a half and Izere was barely a year old. They were being taken care of by our house-maid, who had managed to struggle into the camp. Both of the children were covered in dirt and appeared to be starving and barely alive. They had been living for months on ground-up chicken feed. Where were their parents? Tatiana was frantic to know. But the maid could only hold up her hands. The parents had both disappeared shortly after the genocide broke out. I remember shaking hands with my brother-in-law and his wife the night of the president's assassination, a time that seemed to be as far away as my own childhood. He was bidding me good-bye and urged me to be safe before I went into my house that night. I now wondered if I had shaken his hand for the last time.

There were stories like that all over the camp: unexpected reunions and revelations of awful news from the past two and a half months. Nights were the hardest for us. Weeping filled the air. I found it hard to find even the mindless release of sleep. Wives came to understand that they would never see their missing husbands again. Parents had to force themselves to stop imagining how their irreplaceable children had died at the hands of strangers. And that emptiness in their lives would go on and on. It took a tremendous force of will to keep your own heart together in this unending grief.

The rebel soldiers were hardly welcoming. They treated us like prisoners of war. Some of the stronger men among us were offered the chance to take a few days of military training to fight against the Rwandan Army. The offer was a little tempting, but I refused. "I always fight with words," I told them. "Not with guns." Many of the refugees who chose to join up never came back; they were killed in combat, or killed by their supposed protectors in the rebel army. They were invited for meetings and that was their last night on earth.

What I really wanted was to get the hell out of Rwanda. I had had enough. We were away from the militias but still in danger to be killed anytime by the rebels. We were also filthy and exhausted and needing a break. I told my new hosts that I and my family wanted either to be driven to the Ugandan border or flown to Belgium. What I got in reply was a wishy-washy response, that classic *Rwandan no* of which I was thoroughly sick: "We will look into it for you, Mr. Manager." Nothing happened, of course. Day followed day. All we could do was eat more purloined bananas and wait for the war to be over, or to be killed ourselves.

Meanwhile, one of the largest mass migrations of people in African history was under way.

The government of France had been in continual and friendly contact with its allies at the top of the Hutu government and was growing increasingly alarmed at the likelihood of their neocolony falling to English-speaking rebels. In mid-June, just as my hotel was being evacuated, the French announced plans to send a peacekeeping mission to the western part of Rwanda for "humanitarian" reasons. This gave the *génocidaires* the chance to look like victims instead of aggressors, and they started to pack up and leave for the protected area that became known as "the Turquoise Zone."

RTLM radio then performed its final disservice to the nation by scaring the living daylights out of the people remaining in Rwanda, a considerable number of whom had just spent two months murdering their neighbors and chasing the less compliant ones through swamps. The radio told them that the RPF would kill any Hutus they found in their path and encouraged all its listeners to pack up their belongings and head either to Tanzania or the western part of the country and the borders of the Democratic Republic of Congo (what used to be called Zaire), where the French soldiers awaited. Nearly 1.7 million people heeded the call. Entire hills and cities mobilized into caravans: men carrying sacks of bananas, some with bloody machetes in their belt loops; women with baskets of grain on their heads; children hugging photo albums to their chests. They wound their way past corpses piled at the side of the road and the smoldering cooking fires in front of looted houses. I am sorry to say that the dire predictions of the radio were not rooted in fantasy, as the rebels did conduct crimes against humanity in revenge for the genocide and to make people fear them. In any case, what was left of Rwanda emptied out within days.

The U.N. Security Council, so ineffective in the face of the genocide, lent its sponsorship to the camps the French set up to protect the "refugees." The main place of comfort to the killers was at a town called Goma, just over the border into the Democratic Republic of Congo. It is in a bleak area at the foot of a chain of volcanoes and the town is set in a plain of hardened black lava. Into this hellish landscape, the French airlifted twenty-five hundred well-equipped paratroopers, Foreign

Legionnaires, helicopters, fighter jets, tents, water supplies, food, jeeps—everything, in short, that the pathetic UN force could have used when the murders were at their height in April. Now all of these assets were being used to feed and shelter some of the very people who carried out the slaughter.

Many of the French troops sent to support the effort were apparently there in the belief that they would eventually be used to attack the rebel army, which was closing in on Kigali. Meanwhile, the *Interahamwe* began organizing the refugees into squadrons in the camps, preparing them for an imminent return to Rwanda to keep filling the graves. Radio RTLM set up relay transmitters in the camp so their broadcasts could continue to be heard among the faithful. It was difficult to tell the innocent from the guilty, but comfort was provided to everyone.

In a surprise for all of us the United States finally was persuaded to act. When cholera and other diseases broke out the Clinton administration announced it would seek $320 million in aid for the camps at Goma and the killers and announced a public health initiative to clean up the water-bloated corpses that had floated over into Uganda. This US aid package totaled more than sixteen times what it would have taken to electronically jam the hate radio, which would have stopped many of those people from becoming corpses.

On July 4, with much of the civilian population in flight, the RPF captured the capital of Kigali after a brief battle. They had conquered a ruined city and caused further destruction. Houses were knocked over. Churches were covered in blood. Hospitals were empty shells, looted of supplies. Land mines and live mortar rounds were lying everywhere. Wrecked vehicles blocked the roads. And the corpses were stuffed everywhere: inside closets, underneath desks, and down water wells, and shoved casually to the edge of the sidewalks. The stench of decaying flesh choked the air. Barely thirty thousand people remained, a tenth of Kigali's population before the genocide began.

Rwanda's other major cities toppled swiftly from there and the country was all but conquered. On July 14 the plug was pulled on RTLM for good. Less than a week later the rebel army swore in a new government. It marked the official end of the genocide, but not the end of the killings. The aftermath would be long and dirty.

I was informed that my request to travel to Belgium had been approved on one condition: that I travel alone, leaving my wife and children behind. "Forget it," I told them. "I have changed my mind. I am staying now."

The rebel army took us back to the Mille Collines, which was in wretched shape. After I had left some people had taken it upon themselves to start cooking fires on the lobby tiles and ash was everywhere. The hallway carpets were covered in a disgusting glaze of grease and human waste. Doors were broken from their hinges. The RPF had looted the remaining supply of drinks and liquor that I had used to keep so many people alive. The kitchen was a disaster. Almost everything of value had been stolen or damaged beyond repair.

I cleared the squatters out, rallied what staff I could find, and got to work. We obtained some cleaning solution and carpentry equipment to make the place semipresentable again. My colleague Bik Cornelis had arrived back in the country from the Netherlands and was working side by side with me. The hotel had to start functioning again. Rwanda was about to be besieged with journalists, humanitarian workers, peacekeeping soldiers, and more than 150 nongovernmental organizations. All those people who had abandoned us during the slaughter were coming back and they needed a place to stay. The irony was too bitter to think of for long. There were many things it didn't pay to think of for very long. And truthfully, it felt good just to have this housekeeping task in front of me, and I lost myself in a million details. I am a hotel manager and this was where I belonged.

We reopened on July 15, having been closed a little less than a month.

My family settled in the manager's house at the Hotel Diplomates, where some of our friends had hidden under the noses of the *génocidaires*. It was where we felt the safest. We did not dare to go back to our family house in Kabeza, and I had no particular desire to see those neighbors of mine who had transformed themselves into lunatics during those first days in April.

My wife and I had been continually worried about our families in the south and I was able to take a day off from the hotel to go check on them. My friend John Bosco hot-wired an abandoned car, as was the custom in those days immediately after the genocide. When the road opened up into the lush hills that I loved, we found ourselves in a twilight country we did not recognize. The silence was near complete. Everybody was either dead or exiled. The only thing I heard was dogs barking and snarling as they fought each other to feast on human remains. Crowds of people normally line the sides of the roads in Rwanda: boys driving herds of goats; women in colorful shifts balancing baskets on their heads; elderly men carrying sticks and wearing donated T-shirts; merchants hawking batteries and leaves of tobacco on blankets spread on the ground. They were nowhere to be seen. The life of the country had been sucked away. It was like a plague from the Dark Ages had descended.

"I don't know this place," said my wife. "I'm scared."

I began to dislike the eucalyptus trees on the side of the highway. They were reminding me of the killers I'd seen from the hotel roof. I found myself scanning the brush on the side of the road for the flash of a machete or a grinning killer. We saw so many dead bodies scattered on the side of the road that we began not to see them anymore. I wanted to make conversation with my wife just to distract myself, but there was nothing to talk about that didn't lead to a bad place, and so I fell into a reverie. I wondered how many of those dead shells I might have known in the time before, perhaps people who had come into the Mille Collines for drinks, or relatives of friends that I'd met. Perhaps I'd only passed them in the markets without looking. Whoever they were, each one was irreplaceable, as irreplaceable to the people they loved as I was to my wife, or she was to me, or us to our children. Their uniqueness was gone forever, their stories, their experiences, their loves—erased with a few swings of a cheap machete.

Ah, Rwanda. Why?

My family and I could easily have been a part of that caravan of the dead. All it would have taken was a slip of my luck, the wrong word to a general, a whim of a militia chief. Even after everything I had seen in the previous three months I felt as though I had been terribly naive. I hadn't really grasped the true scale of the disaster, how deep it had gone, and how that membrane of protection around our hotel had been so fragile. That it had held up for seventy-six days was a miracle. With the rest of the country looking like a giant cemetery there was nothing that should have stopped those killers from wiping us out as well. We would have been like a handful of sand on a mile-long beach.

It did not ease my feeling of general anxiety at all that we were the only car on the road. There were a number of roadblocks, of course. They were manned not by the *Interahamwe* this time, but by the RPF. The soldiers looked at us curiously. "What are you doing out here?" they wanted to know. "Don't you know how dangerous it is out here?" They were very suspicious of us. But they let us pass.

We arrived in my hometown after a few hours. It was as deserted as the roads had been. This was where my friend Aloise had wanted us to take refuge—the place where the *mwami* had taken his cows for safety during wars of past centuries. But that old myth had been broken in the past few weeks. The genocide had come here, too. More than 150 people connected to the Seventh-day Adventist Church had had the same idea as Aloise. These rural pastors and their families had come here thinking they would be protected at the college at Gitwe where I had attended school. They had all been slaughtered.

It occurred to me that if I had stayed with my earlier ambition to be a pastor, I might very well have been among them, and then killed in the same classroom where I had learned to make letters.

Things were no better in the neighboring town where my family had lived. In the commune house several dozen Tutsis had gathered under the protection of the local mayor, who had promised to shield them from the mobs of ordinary people who had taken up machetes against their neighbors. On April 18 an official had been called to a political meeting in the nearby city of Gitarama, and when he came back there was trouble. "I am no longer the person you knew," he allegedly said, and then put a handgun to the head of a friend of his, a man he had gone to school with and had known for more than twenty years. He shot his friend and then ordered an attack on the commune house. Those refugees who weren't killed immediately darted into the swamps and the hills, where they spent the next two months trying to hide from the bands of bar keepers, schoolteachers, and housewives who had been told: "Do your work."

I went to the home of my elder brother Munyakayanza and found him sitting quietly in the front room with his wife. Seeing him alive made me want to cry with gratitude. We embraced, but I could feel that his muscles were tense. His eyes darted from my eyes to the places behind my shoulder. The area around his house was usually full of life, neighbors passing back and forth, children rolling bicycle rims with sticks, and teenagers playing tussling games, but now there was nobody. Not even any cooking fires were burning. It was totally quiet.

"Our neighbors have been killed by the militia," he told me. He and his wife survived because they were Hutus. Now that the rebel army had driven out the militia it was not safe anymore to be of this class. In fact, it could be a death sentence. Some rogue members of the RPF had begun to conduct reprisal killings in several parts of Rwanda. Around me I could see burned-out houses where people had been roasted alive within their own walls.

"Listen, brother," Munyakayanza told me. "Please leave this place. The houses, they have eyes. The trees have ears."

I decoded his message. My presence here would be noticed and was a danger to both his family and mine. I quickly hugged him again and left. My wife started to cry, and I tried my best to comfort her, but it was impossible. We now headed toward my wife's hometown, the old Tutsi capital of Nyanza. Tatiana was so frightened she could barely speak, but we had to see, we had to go there, even though we already knew in our hearts what we would find.

Most of her family had been slain by their neighbors. Several of them had been buried in a shallow pit used for the maturing of bananas. Tatiana's mother had been one of the sweetest, kindest women I'd ever met. She had always shared food with her neighbors in times of trouble and was always available to help look after children in their parents' absence. She had been murdered along with her daughter-in-law and six grandchildren. The walls of her house had been knocked down. I could see some of its distinctive tiles already plastered into the walls of nearby houses. The looting had been quick and efficient.

I felt bright hatred surging up in my throat for the bastards that had done this. I am not a violent man, but if I had had a gun in that moment, and if somebody had pointed me to a convincing scapegoat, I would have murdered him without hesitation. I had saved more than a thousand people in the capital, but I could not save my own family. What a stupid and useless man I was!

I tasted, in that moment, the poison and self-hatred in my country's bloodstream, that irresistible fury against a ghost, the quenchless desire to make someone pay for an unrightable wrong. My father would have said that I had drunk from the water that was upstream from the lamb.

My wife and I crouched there in the remains of her mother's house, holding on to each other, and for the first time in many years, I wept.

Nothing could ever be the same for us again.

My family and I stayed in the manager's cottage at the Diplomates while Rwanda went about the slow process of trying to rebuild itself. Work is an excellent place to lose yourself, and I proceeded to do just that. My bosses at Sabena had been satisfied with my performance during the genocide, and I was allowed to keep my job as the general manager of the Hotel Diplomates. Business was booming, of course. Rwanda's expatriate class had swelled once again now that the terror was over.

There was a change in my employment in February 1995.

The Sabena Corporation was planning to merge with Swissair, but a condition of the deal was that Sabena would renovate all of its existing hotels. They were then forced to break their management contract with the new government of Rwanda, which was the legal owner of the Diplomates. This put me in a difficult spot. I thought about asking for another job in the corporation, but I enjoyed too much the demands of day-to-day management—the attending of the thousand little details that make a hotel the welcoming place that it is. This was my deepest image of myself. I was born to be a site manager, not a suit in a conference room. And so Sabena and I parted on friendly terms.

But I found a way to stay on as the manager of the Diplomates. With the Belgian corporation now gone the government needed someone experienced to run the hotel and I brought them a proposal that allowed me to stay on as manager while still living on the property. My wife opened a pharmacy downtown and we managed to make a decent living together while Rwanda tried to reinvent itself as a new nation.

The government got rid of those wretched ID books and made it taboo for anyone to be officially labeled as a Hutu or a Tutsi—a change that I and millions of others applauded. Informal "orphanages" spontaneously opened up all over the country, often run by teenagers; few adults were left to take charge. An entire generation of young people was told never to mention their ethnicity to anyone because it could mark them for death in the changing currents of history. Rwandan exiles from all over the world, some of whom hadn't seen their country for thirty years, flooded back inside. There were more than three-quarters of a million of them, which meant there were roughly three new settlers for every four people who had been killed in the genocide, a ghoulish impersonal replacement. The exiles were mostly from Uganda, Burundi and the Congo, but they came from the United States and Canada and Belgium and Switzerland as well. Prisons, meanwhile, were jammed full of people suspected of having killed their neighbors.

The economy, like the infrastructure, was in a shambles. An entire year's coffee crop had been lost. What little industry there was had been destroyed. But international aid helped get the power back on, and Rwandans have always been creative when it comes to making money. There was a brief period of Wild West capitalism, in which it became possible to grow very rich transporting foodstuffs and goods from Uganda. Anybody with a working truck could make fantastic profits hauling bananas and beans.

My own life, meanwhile, became complicated and a little frightening. It was with profoundly mixed feelings that I returned to the streets where I had seen the bodies of my friends and neighbors stacked up like garbage. Their bloodstains had washed away in the autumn rains, but I always took note of the spots where I had seen them lying.

The Mille Collines no longer smelled like a refugee camp, but it was hard to walk its halls without feeling that palpable sense of impending murder. The role I had played in saving those people had not been forgotten, and it was not appreciated in many quarters. I had seen too much and knew too many names. There were many people in the new government who had been complicit in the genocide and who feared any surviving witnesses from that time. They were political survivors, hard men, dangerous when threatened. Every time I saw a stranger scowl in my direction I tried to memorize his face in case I had to find him later if he harmed my family.

Others had it in for me for economic reasons. The hotel management contract I had received was seen as a cash cow by some of the thugs close to the new government. One very bizarre incident at the hotel convinced me I might be better off living someplace else. A friend of mine came by the hotel one evening with an Army sergeant. The sergeant was highly agitated and it became clear that my friend was not there by choice. I tried to calm things down and offered them a beer, but the sergeant would not sit still for long. He took out his pistol and told me: "We know you have stolen computers in your house!"

"That is foolish," I told him.

"Then you will not have any problem showing me your house?"

"All right," I said. "This is foolishness, but if you insist, come look."

The three of us walked into the next room. Our housemaid was inside, and when she saw the Army sergeant's pistol, she screamed.

"He is going to kill you!" she said, and without thinking, I dashed toward the sergeant and shoved him hard into the wall. He dropped his gun. I supposed I could have grabbed it off the floor and pointed it at him, but my instinct told me otherwise. I raced out into the parking lot and toward the Army post next door—the place, as it happened, where the ten Belgian soldiers had been killed by torture in the opening hours of the genocide. There is hardly a patch of ground in Rwanda, of course, where *somebody* was not hacked to death in 1994. I got the attention of some of the soldiers on guard and told them I had been threatened by the sergeant. They took him away and I learned that he was attached to the Department of Military Intelligence, our nation's version of the CIA.

The next day, an influential Army major named Rwabalinda came in to see me about the incident.

"Mr. Manager, that man did not have a real gun. It was a toy."

I could not believe what I was hearing. If the major was concocting a story about what had happened it meant that there were some high-ranking people who wanted to see me gone.

"Listen, major," I told him. "I am not a solider and I don't even like guns, but I know the difference between a real gun and a toy. That sergeant was carrying a real gun."

"It was not. This is what our investigation has shown."

I thought it best to keep a stone face. I thanked the major and he left. Shortly thereafter a friend high up in the government, who I should not identify, came to my house and made plain what I already knew to be true.

"Paul, I have heard they want to kill you so that other business interests can take over the management of the Hotel Diplomates," he said. "But the object now is not to kill you out in the open. It is too dangerous politically. They will pretend they are arresting you and taking you to prison, but you will disappear and your body will never be found."

The choice now seemed clear to me. I could open up my treasured black binder once again and start dialing all my Army friends for protection. But it would be like living the genocide all over. Years ago I had looked forward into my future as a church pastor and seen nothing but rural banality waiting for me. Now I imagined my future as a Rwandan hotel manager and saw nothing but constant fear and an eventual knock on the door after midnight. I loved my job and I loved my country, but not enough to die for them and leave my children without a father. My family and I quickly flew to Belgium and applied for political asylum. We had remained in our own country slightly more than two years after the genocide.

We may have left Rwanda, but Rwanda will never leave us. Those thousand hills were imprinted inside us forever. There are times today when I walk down a street and smell a fire burning in a hearth and instantly I am back in Nkomera, and it is evening, and my father is coming back from the village with a butchered goat on his back and my mother has lit the fire for supper and the shadows of the banana trees are long on the hillsides.

And there are times when I will be in some public place, in a small crowd at a bus station, for example, and I suddenly cannot bear the presence of the other people because I see them holding machetes. They are always grinning at me.

Tatiana and my children have similar troubles and it is not uncommon for one of us to awake screaming in the middle of the night. When this happens I always come in and hold whoever it is, and we talk in quiet voices, in Kinyarwanda, until calm comes once more. It is the best therapy, I think, to simply talk about the things you have seen, and we have talked hundreds of times together about the dreadful things we have lived through. We will probably be talking about them together as long as we are alive, a conversation that will never end.

It is not such a bad thing to start one's life afresh. I was forty-two years old. We had a lot of bad memories, but we were all in good physical health and we all had hope for a better life in our new country. I had always liked going to Belgium on vacation and it would be free of the violence and fear that I wanted to be done with forever. As a twentieth-century colonial power Belgium had done wretched things to Rwanda, and its conduct during the recent genocide was not honorable, but I never held the actions of its government against the people at large, who were generally very likable and decent to me.

Belgium has a very generous social service net for its citizens, and even for the recent immigrants, but I felt very strongly that I did not want to live on public assistance or take any kind of handout. I was restless and eager to go to work. Since managing a hotel was not in the cards for me anymore, I decided to become another kind of manager. I had a little cash saved up from the Diplomates contract and I used twenty thousand dollars of it to buy a Nissan car and a permit to run a taxi company. The city of Brussels requires you to take an exam to be a taxi driver and I passed on the first try. I was now a company with one employee: myself. There is a saying in Rwanda: "If you want to own cows you must sleep in the fields with them." In other words, money comes only with long workdays. So I started going to work at 5:00 A.M. and coming home at 7:00 P.M. The streets in Brussels are tangled like spaghetti, and many switch their names after only a few blocks, but I quickly learned the major arteries and then started to master the side streets. I cruised all over the city dozens of times in a day, usually with a stranger in the backseat, a businessperson usually, or somebody with dealings at the European Community headquarters.

Most of the people who were in my cab for more than half an hour became my friends. Quite a few were talkative people and would want to know the name of my home country. When I told them "Rwanda" it usually led into conversations about the genocide, which most everyone had heard about. I was occasionally not in the mood to talk about it, but on most days I was, and I would answer their questions as best I could. There were just a handful of passengers, on very long rides, who got to hear me tell the story of the Hotel Mille Collines, and they always left my cab in silence.

Sometimes very early in the mornings, when the sun was not yet up, I would cruise on the cobblestones of the Place des Palais, past the antique lamps in front of the neoclassical Royal Palace where King Leopold II had lived in the early part of the twentieth century. His monarchy had been propped up and financed by the occupation of the Congo and the fantastic profits from rubber exports. But his agents had used terrible force to collect the rubber from the Africans and had instituted an economy that was slavery in all but name. They were known for chopping the hands from able-bodied men who failed to make their quotas. Their colleagues had not been so systematically brutal in Rwanda, but they were the instigators of the divide-and-conquer strategy that turned Hutu against Tutsi, brother against brother, all for the sake of profit.

The profits had come to this marbled jewel of a city, and I circled around it in my taxicab, alone, looking for anyone who might need a ride.

There is not much left to tell about my new life in Belgium. My wife and I made some friends from Rwanda—fellow postgenocide immigrants like us—and they have their own stories to tell. When the evening is late and the empty glasses multiply on the coffee table, we will sometimes talk about what we have seen with each other, and there will be crying and gentle embraces. We have friends among other Rwandans who have lived here a long time and were fortunate enough to be elsewhere when the killing started. One thing is unique among these expatriates: We haven't the slightest regard for each other's status as a Hutu or a Tutsi. I think the shared experience of being a stranger in a semistrange land makes us all just Rwandans, and for that I am proud of my countrymen.

About fifteen thousand of us now make the old colonial capital our home, and there are a few specialty stores where we can buy goods that remind us of where we came from. We go to each other's baptisms, marriages, and funerals and it is enormously good for us to hear Kinyarwanda and drink beer with others who understand us in a way that the Belgians never can. These events usually go on well into the evening and are accompanied by hours of talk, laughter, and dancing. I suppose these are ordinary enough rituals for an immigrant, but it means so much to me to feel that connection with my old country.

But as Rwanda will always be with me, so too will the genocide. It is as much a part of me as the shade of my eyes or the names of my children; it is never far from my thoughts and I cannot talk for more than one hour with a fellow Rwandan before one or both of us will begin to tell a story or make a reference to what happened during those three months of blood in 1994. It is the darkest bead on our national necklace, and one we all must wear, no matter how far we have traveled to get away. Killers still walk free in Rwanda and in the world, and through my mind. I remember one evening in Brussels, at a banquet after someone's wedding, when I saw a familiar face in the crowd. It was a man I hadn't seen in years, a Hutu neighbor of mine from the Kabeza neighborhood where my family and I had lived. I had seen him in the opening days of the genocide wearing an Army uniform and carrying a machete. It seems likely that he participated in some murders, or at a minimum did nothing to stop them. And here he was, free and healthy and wearing a business suit. There was nothing I could do about it, either. I stared into my drink. My wife wondered why I had suddenly gone quiet, but I could not tell her until we had gone home. I did not want to talk to this man. I never wanted to see him again, and so far I have not.

These banquets we have together frequently take place in the rented basements of various churches around Brussels. Church is not an uncomfortable place for me to be, but I rarely go to worship on my own. My wife is still a faithful Catholic, but I am what you might call a lapsed Seventh-day Adventist. It was enormously disappointing to me that so many priests and pastors caught the hateful virus in 1994 and refused to do anything for those who were begging them for help. The church remained mostly silent when it should have been speaking out in a loud voice. Its failure to stand strong in this critical hour was equivalent to complicity. It still disturbs me that houses of prayer could have been transformed into killing zones.

I still believe in a kind of Higher Power that is the origin of all we see around us, but I am not one who prays much anymore. I felt that God left me on my own during the genocide. I have many troubling questions that I fear will go unanswered until the day I die. I share this yearning in the heart with many other Rwandans. Was God hiding from us during the killing? It used to be that God and I shared many drinks together as friends. We don't talk much anymore, but I would like to think that we can one day reconcile over an *urwagwa* and he will explain everything to me. But that time is not yet here.

Some of those people who lived through the genocide with me have gone on to what might be called happiness, or at least a future without too much pain or fear. Odette Nyiramilimo became close to the new government and was appointed to secretary of state for the Department of Social Affairs. She is now a senator in the Parliament of Rwanda. Her husband, Jean-Baptiste, reopened his clinic in the heart of Kigali and continues to see patients every day. My journalist friend Thomas Kamilindi took a job with the British Broadcasting Company as a correspondent in Rwanda, where his honest and unflinching news reports continued to irritate those in power. He recently accepted a fellowship at the University of Michigan.

For others, the future was bleak. My other journalist friend Edward Mutsinzi, who swore a blood oath in Room 126 to protect my children, was captured and tortured by RPF soldiers shortly after the liberation of Kigali. For some reason, they thought he had useful information. They beat him to a pulp and left him for dead. A squad of Australian soldiers attached to the United Nations found him lying in the dirt and helped save his life. He lives today in Belgium, blind and unable to work. Another man who swore that oath with me, John Bosco Karangwa, grew sick and died in 2001. His wife and children live nearby and I visit them when I can.

Aloise Karasankwavu, the bank executive who tried to persuade me to flee with him to Murama, wanted to help rebuild my country at the end of the civil war. He had just passed an exam to be the director of one of the nation's largest banks, BCDI, when he was thrown in jail on bogus charges of helping carry out the genocide. He died in his cell one night of suspicious causes. No autopsy was performed.

The top architects of the genocide have mostly been rounded up and taken before the International Criminal Tribunal in Tanzania. The colonel accused of planning the genocide, Theoneste Bagosora, is still on trial as I write this. So is the head of the national police, Augustin Ndindiliyimana. My friend Georges Rutaganda, the vice president of the *Interahamwe* and the main supplier of beer and toilet paper to the Mille Collines, was sentenced to life imprisonment for crimes against humanity in 1999. He was specifically charged, among other things, with organizing the massacre at the Official Technical School where the killings began minutes after the UN jeeps disappeared down the road. As for the priest who wore a gun instead of his robes, Father Wenceslas Munyeshyaka, he now lives in exile in France. A judge there brought charges against him in 1995 for the crime of genocide. His case is still caught in the slow gears of the French judicial system and may never be resolved.

I have no idea what happened to that neighbor of mine I called Marcel, the clerk I saw wearing a military uniform and carrying a machete on the morning of April 7, 1994. As far as I know, he has melted back into a normal life and is now going to work, paying his taxes, and raising his children.

General Romeo Dallaire suffered emotional stress and was voluntarily relieved of his command the month after the end of the war. Back in Canada, he wrestled with posttraumatic stress disorder and was found one night in 1997 curled in a fetal position under a park bench, drunk and incoherent. Dallaire has since found a new life as an author and a lecturer and is now a fellow at the John F. Kennedy School of Government at Harvard University. His old boss, Kofi Annan, is now the secretary-general of the United Nations.

President Bill Clinton stopped over in Rwanda on March 25, 1998, and offered an apology for America's failure to intervene. He stayed for approximately three hours and did not leave the airport.

The daughters of Tatiana's brother now live in our home in Brussels. We raised them as our own children and they are both healthy and doing well in school. They have no memories of the violence and the awful ordeal they had been through, for which I am grateful. But they will never know their parents. My brother-in-law and his wife vanished without a trace after that first night when the president was assassinated. We can only assume they were slaughtered and their bodies are now in an anonymous mass grave somewhere. I hope their ending came without much suffering, and I also hope that wherever they are they might know what lovely girls their babies would one day become.

Our relatives in Rwanda tried the best they could to begin life anew. They still raise cows and bananas in the hills near Nyanza. We decided not to remove my mother-in-law and her grandchildren from the banana pit where they had been buried, but placed a memorial stone on top of it instead. I can only hope they are resting in peace wherever they are. The house knocked over by the militia was never rebuilt. A pile of rubble stands there today and weeds grow over it. As for my own family, I have lost four of my eight siblings. One died of illness, one died in a car accident, and two were killed by the rebel army. For a Rwandan family, this is a comparatively lucky outcome.

My children sometimes ask me why it all happened and I don't have any final answers for them. The only thing I am able to do is to keep talking to them about what they have seen and how they feel about it. I will listen to them for hours and hours into the night, and sometimes they listen to me and my own bad memories. Roger and I both know, for example, what it is like to face a former friend across the divide of ethnicity. And all of us know what it is like to see people we knew stacked in heaps by the side of the road and to feel that awful helplessness in the face of evil. I did not grow up with any understanding of modern psychology, but I do feel the best way to get rid of bad memories is to speak them out loud and not keep them fermenting inside. It is the best therapy. Words can be instruments of evil, but they can also be powerful tools of life. If you say the right ones they can save the whole world. I thank God that my own father never had to experience the genocide and see the hatefulness in the heart of his country, but

I also think he would have known how to use words against the darkness that comes and keeps coming long after the killing is over.

With hard work and a lot of early mornings I earned enough money to buy a second taxi—this one was a Mitsubishi—and hire another driver. The cash flow was slow but steady, and I eventually accumulated enough capital to branch out. I felt strongly that I wanted to invest in Africa. But Rwanda was not a possibility because I could not travel freely there. Through some friends I learned of an opportunity to buy into a trucking company in the nation of Zambia, a former British colony many miles south of Rwanda. It is an English-speaking country, so I am able to do business there easily. We now have a fleet of four trucks that haul canned goods, beer, soda, and clothing to rural villages from the capital city of Lusaka. Our trucks can haul most anything imaginable, and it always makes me happy to sign a contract with an international aid organization bringing something to a needy area.

My income was good enough for us to buy a slim postwar town house just fifty meters outside the city limits of Brussels proper. It is something of a joke among my friends that I take such pride in this geographical detail, for it allows me to say I live in a "suburb of Brussels." After so much angst as a young man over the idea of living in a city I have finally come to rest in suburbia. Diane married a man who works for a company that manufactures hospital equipment and Lys married a self-employed businessman. Roger has gone to work for Accor hotels and may one day become a manager like his father. Tresor is still in school. In the afternoons I drive him to his soccer games and we practice his English in the car. It is getting quite good. I keep trying to lose weight, but I have a taste for steak and potatoes and the French wines whose names and qualities I first learned in college. My doctor has told me to stop drinking so much coffee because it makes my blood pressure go up. Most of the time I listen, but sometimes I sneak a cup more than I should. Pictures of my family are on the fireplace mantle, and there is a basketball hoop mounted in the backyard.

All in all it is a contented life, and I want no more adventure in it. I would have been happy to have lived out my remaining time as a good husband to my wife, a decent father to my children, and a safety-conscious driver for my passengers, with what happened at the Hotel Mille Collines only a private memory, a forgotten episode in history. I went through hell and lived to tell the story, but I never expected to tell the story to you quite like this. The way it happened is a brief footnote.

One day in 1999 the telephone rang. On the line was a young man from New York named Keir Pearson who said he was researching a screenplay on the Rwandan genocide. A friend of his had been traveling in Africa at the time and had heard the dramatic radio interview given by my friend Thomas Kamilindi. The young man from New York had borrowed money from his girlfriend to buy an air ticket to Rwanda and wanted to talk to me. I said, sure, come for a visit on your stopover to Kigali. The story of the Mille Collines was already well known. It had been told on the BBC and the Voice of America and other radio programs. But nobody had put it on film.

I spent an hour with Keir Pearson in my town house and was impressed with his sincerity, as well as with his desire to get the story correct. His business partner was an Irish film director named Terry George and together they made the movie *Hotel Rwanda* about my experience. There were a few dramatic embellishments, but I know that's typical for Hollywood movies, and the story was very close to the truth. The movie earned Academy Award nominations for Pearson and George as well as for the two main actors, Sophie Okonedo and Don Cheadle, whom I later befriended. I was happy he was chosen, for he is a fine actor and much better looking than I.

It was very strange for me to be called a "hero" the way that I was when the movie was released in Europe and America. I was invited to the White House to meet President George W. Bush, who told me he saw the movie twice. I started giving lectures about the current state of affairs in Africa today and the importance of truth and reconciliation in the aftermath of genocide. With the help of some friends I started the Hotel

Rwanda Rusesabagina Foundation to provide education and health care to the thousands of orphans and homeless children who live in Rwanda today. Nearly half a million children were left parentless by the murders. The others, the younger ones, are what are known as *enfants du mauvais souvenir,* or "children of bad memories." They are the ones whose mothers were raped, impregnated and left to survive. Quite a few are HIV-positive from birth. Most of them never knew a mother's unconditional love because of the terrible way in which they came into the world. My foundation is dedicated to funding orphanages and medical treatment and to providing education for these lost children so that they may know some hope and not become a part of a future surge of evil in Rwanda. We cannot change the past, but we can improve the future with the limited tools and words that we have been given.

Words are the most powerful tools of all, and especially the words that we pass to those who come after us. I will never forget that favorite saying of my father's: "Whoever does not talk to his father never knows what his grandfather said." So I decided to write this book for the sake of the historic record.

I am a Rwandan, after all, and I know that all things pass away but history. History never dies. It is what defines us as a civilization, and we live out our collective histories every day, in ways both good and evil. Over and over people kept telling me that what I did at the Mille Collines was heroic, but I never saw it that way, and I still don't. I was providing shelter. I was a hotel manager doing his job. That is the best thing anyone can say about me, and all I ever wanted. And that's really the best I have to give.

ELEVEN

IN A VILLAGE SOUTH OF KIGALI is a church that is no longer a church. The compound is surrounded with a low stone wall and the ground is covered with weeds. The building itself is shaped like an auditorium; the walls are of red brick. The floor is poured concrete. The stained-glass windows are cracked and broken. Spatters of grenade fragments are in the walls and the tin ceiling is shot though with hundreds of bullet holes. On sunny days you can see shafts of thin light streaming through, and the spots they make on the floor look like a constellation of stars.

This is the former parish church in the community of Nyamata. The name means "place of milk." The church had been renowned as a safe haven during Rwanda's past troubles. When the killings started in the spring of 1994 the Tutsis of the region were encouraged to hide in the sanctuary. The refugees locked the iron gates and prayed while their friends and neighbors eagerly struggled to break inside to murder them. On April 14 the Presidential Guard was called in from

Kigali and they threw grenades at the gates, blasting them into shards. The ordinary people and the soldiers flooded in and thousands of people were massacred.

The building has since been seized from the Vatican. It is now an official memorial to the genocide, but it functions also as a crypt. There are burlap bags full of skulls in a side room. Some of them bear a slice where a machete chopped into the brain. Out in the backyard is an open tomb with thousands of skeletons, with the skulls arranged in neat rows, the bones stacked up on wooden shelves. Most of them were found in the sanctuary, where the bodies were stacked three deep, but others were recovered from mass graves and pit toilets around the village. The altar is covered with a bloodstained cloth. The back wall has stains on the bricks left by the children whose heads were smashed against it. Quietness reigns.

Standing out front is a sign draped with a purple cloth. It bears a pledge in four languages: "Never Again."

We all know these words. But we never seem to hear them.

What happened? Hitler's Final Solution was supposed to have been the last expression of this monstrous idea—the final time the world would tolerate a deliberate attempt to exterminate an entire race. But genocide remains the most pressing human rights question of the twenty-first century.

Each outbreak has its differences on the surface. In Cambodia slaughter was done in the name of absurd political dogma; in Bosnia the killings erupted after the fragmenting of a multi-ethnic federation; the Kurds in Iraq were gassed when they demanded independence from a dictator; and today in Sudan innocent people are dying because they occupy oil-rich territory coveted by the ethnic majority.

Rwanda had its own unique set of circumstances. We had a radio station that broadcast vicious racial humor—"jokes" that sounded more and more like commands with each telling. We had bad leadership concerned more for its own survival than the needs of the people. We had a long history of grabbing impunity, in which people were allowed to get away with the most flagrant property crimes and job discriminations so long as they were committed against Tutsis. We had a history of tit-for-tat massacres in the countryside that were never investigated. And we had a hungry and desperate population that was taught to see the midnight murder of their neighbors as a potential economic windfall.

Look closely at each of the world's recent genocides, however, and the surface differences burn away. The core of genocide is always the same. They erupt under the cover of a war. They are the brainchildren of insecure leaders eager for more power. Governments ease their people into them gradually. Other nations must be persuaded to look away. And all genocides rely heavily on the power of group thinking to embolden the everyday killers.

This last factor is the most powerful commonality of all, and without it no genocide could take place.

Let me explain what I mean. We were all born with a powerful herd instinct and it can force otherwise rational people to act in inexplicable ways. I would never have believed this to be true if I hadn't seen my own neighbors—gentle, humorous, seemingly normal people—turn into killers in the space of two days. Ordinary citizens, just like you and me, were bullied and cajoled into doing things they would never have dreamed possible without the reinforcing eyes of the group upon them. And in this way murder becomes not just possible but routine. It even gets boring after a while.

The French reporter Jean Hatzfeld earned the trust of ten imprisoned Rwandan murderers, and they described to him the workaday business of human slaughter. "In the end, a man is like an animal; you give him a whack on the head, and down he goes," said one. "In the first days someone who had already slaughtered chickens—and especially goats—had an advantage, understandably. Later, everybody grew accustomed to the new activities and the laggards caught up."

Said another: "At the start of the killings, we worked fast and skimmed along because we were eager. In the middle of the killings, we killed casually. Time and triumph encouraged us to loaf around. At first we could feel more patriotic or more deserving when we managed to catch some fugitives. Later on, those feelings deserted us. We stopped listening to the fine words on the radio and from the authorities. We killed to keep the job going."

It is no surprise to me at all that the young teenagers in the refugee camps could have been organized into *Interahamwe* chapters in the winter of 1993. Something magical happens to you when you join a group, a feeling I can only describe as *freedom*. I felt it myself on various soccer teams when I was growing up. I also felt it when I joined the staff of the Hotel Mille Collines. It is possible to lose oneself in the purpose of the collective effort; we embrace this feeling of being dissolved into something bigger because at our cores we are lonely. We are trapped inside our own skulls. But we thirst for that unity, that lost wholeness that we imagine we had before we were born. That feeling of warm acceptance we get inside a group is addictive; it is one of the most powerful human urges. And when your individuality is dissolved into the will of the pack you then become free to act in any way the pack directs. The thought of acting otherwise becomes as abhorrent as death. We fear the group will withdraw its acceptance from us and we will be cast out and the love will die. We would do almost anything to keep this from happening. Tyrants understand this. They try to point these groups like spears in any direction that serves their aims. If nobody can find it within themselves to stand outside the group and find the inner strength to say no, then the mass of men will easily commit atrocities for the sake of keeping up personal appearances. The lone man is ridiculed and despised, but he is the only one who can stand between humanity and the abyss.

This is by no means a phenomenon confined to Africa. It has happened in every culture on the planet, in every period, and the advancement of civilization has been no protection. The same nation that gave us Goethe and Beethoven also gave us Hitler. There will be others, and perhaps some in unexpected locations, and the only question will be whether uninvolved people have the courage to take a risk to save strangers.

A sad truth of human nature is that it is hard to care for people when they are abstractions, hard to care when it is not you or somebody close to you. Unless the world community can stop finding ways to dither in the face of this monstrous threat to humanity those words *Never Again* will persist in being one of the most abused phrases in the English language and one of the greatest lies of our time.

I am sometimes asked to name the thing that most scares me about Rwanda. My answer is this: It frightens me to death when my countrymen are not talking. If a Rwandan is brooding you never know what he is thinking. When I was a hotel manager I made it one of my number-one priorities to talk with just about everybody who came and stayed with us or drank with us. It was one way I kept myself informed of what was brewing in my country. To stay away from evil people is to never know what is on their minds. And it frightens me that my country today is packed with a lot of angry people not talking to each other. We could be witnessing the roots of a future holocaust.

Europe needed the catharsis of its Nuremberg before it could have the renewal of its Marshall Plan. My country has had neither justice nor effective reconstruction. We are not sitting around a table and talking to each other.

For one thing, the pace of the criminal justice system has been painfully slow. At this writing, more than a decade after the genocide, only about twenty-five top government officials have been tried by the United Nations' International Criminal Tribunal in Arusha. Those men are locked up in comfort, which is more than can be said for those ordinary laborers of the genocide who pass their days in squalid misery. Jails in Rwanda are wretched places, not much better than the shipping containers in which some prisoners were kept in the days immediately after the genocide. Facilities are drastically overcrowded, with barely enough room for some of the accused to sit up in bed. There is little to eat, so the relatives of some of the prisoners live around the fringes of these hellholes to bring them food. Although it would be easy to escape almost nobody chooses to, for they would live out their days branded as a murderer, whether true or not. Most of these people actually *want* to be tried. Being thrown in jail for a genocide-related crime in Rwanda does not take much evidence. It sometimes requires merely the accusation of a single person whose motives may not be honest.

Rwanda is attempting to deal with this unique problem in a unique way—by blending traditional notions of justice with a modern court apparatus. The idea is to reconstitute the old village justice system of *gacaca*—justice on the grass—the court of reconciliation so well known by my father. Genocide suspects would be tried and sentenced by their neighbors in small villages across the nation. Farmers and tavern keepers and housewives would be trained to be apprentice judges and lawyers. There are now nearly ten thousand of these courts operating all over the country. I would call it a noble idea. I would also call it a total failure.

Justice on the grass was never designed to address something as grave as genocide. It was designed to solve cases of missing goats and stolen bananas. Serious felony crimes were *always* referred to the courts of the king, even in the days of my grandfather's grandfather. I am a defender of the wisdom of the common man, but it is fantasy to expect a village of laypeople—with their own layers of local intrigue, jealousies, and loyalties—to effectively mete out real justice for something as horrid and earthshaking as mass murder. It would be like taking a rapist to a traffic magistrate. That such a flimsy system has been developed to handle genocide crimes serves only to trivialize the genocide. It insults the dead.

For another thing, the entire point of *gacaca* was not punishment but reconciliation. You were supposed to apologize to the man you had wronged and share a bowl of banana beer as a sign of renewed friendship. But how in God's name can a man "reconcile" with people he has raped, tortured, and murdered? How can things ever be put right with the parents of a baby who has been ripped limb from limb? *Gacaca* is a well-intentioned idea but punishing crimes of genocide requires the authority, stature, and rigor of a state-sponsored court with impartial judges and firm rules of evidence.

The irony is that we could have been a long way down that road if we had had the discipline. After the genocide we still had two hundred state courthouses, known as tribunals, in various locations around Rwanda. Judges were initially hard to find because many had been killed or jailed or fled the country, but the ministry of justice was ready to start trying cases in the spring of 1995. But the Army stopped the first trials and the hearings did not resume for two years, which passed agonizingly slowly for those with nothing to do but look at the patterns of the sun on jailhouse walls. Justice has been a stop-and-start trickle like this ever since. And the waiting goes on for the accused, as does the mounting anger.

This failure of justice is critical, for it leaves our nation still in pieces and in danger of exploding again before long. Breaking the cycle will not be easy. It requires the application of true justice. Without justice there will be more massacres, for widespread injustice never fades away. It ferments and stinks and eventually bursts into bloody flowers.

I am convinced that one of the strongest engines of the Rwandan genocide was the culture of impunity that was allowed to flourish after the revolution against the colonists began in 1959. Rwandans killed their neighbors just to take their houses, people killed people for their banana trees, people leaped over the counters of abandoned general stores and started selling the merchandise as if they were the rightful owners. It was a huge mistake for our government to let this blatant larceny go unanswered. Even today there are people living in houses that don't belong to them and selling merchandise they never bought. This is what I call impunity. A person's private property may seem like a small thing when held in balance against their life, but the success of a small crime grants a kind of permission to carry out worse deeds. It is like that famous American parable about a row of windows in an abandoned factory. If they stay intact nobody will throw rocks at them. But if one window is broken and goes unrepaired, the rest will get shattered by vandals in quick succession, because the public gets the idea that nobody cares about the windows. A sense of social disorder creates more chaos. As a nation we did not care about our windows forty-seven years ago, and I am afraid we are not taking good care of them now.

Another problem is the current government of Rwanda. To

its great credit it has taken steps to stop the identification of anybody as a Hutu or a Tutsi. In many parts of Rwanda today it is now considered rude to discuss somebody's heritage, and this is a good thing. But the changes have gone no further. Rwanda is a country that has still never known democracy. The current president, Paul Kagame, was the general of the Rwandan Patriotic Front army that toppled the *génocidaire* regime and ended the slaughter, and for this he deserves credit. But he has exhibited many characteristics of the classic African strongman ever since taking power. In 2003 he was reelected with 95 percent of the vote. There is nobody in the world that can call results like that a "free election" and keep a straight face.

Moreover, the popular image persists that Rwanda is today a nation governed by and for the benefit of a small group of elite Tutsis. Kagame's government has done little to show the world a different picture. The Parliament is widely known to be a rubber stamp for the will of the president. Those few Hutus who have been elevated to high-ranking posts are usually empty suits without any real authority of their own. They are known locally as *Hutus de service,* or "Hutus for hire." So there is no real sharing of power. What exists now in Rwanda is a new version of the *akazu,* or the "little house" of corrupt businessmen who have long surrounded the president. The same kind of impunity that festered after the 1959 revolution is happening again, only with a different race-based elite in power. We have changed the dancers but the music remains the same.

I said earlier that what my country needs most of all is to sit together around a table and talk. Perhaps we will not talk as the best of friends, not yet, but at least as people with a common history who can respect each other. That discussion never happened, not once in Rwandan history. The dictates of the *mwami* were followed by the plunder of the country by Belgians and then the corrupt ethnic visions of Habyarimana, with the balance of power always bouncing back and forth between the races, and neither side learning *anything* from the ashes and the bodies. We never talk about it; we just steal what we can whenever our turn comes around.

The way that modern nations have that discussion around a table is through the democratic process and the civilized exchange of ideas in a respectful format. But Rwanda has a cosmetic democracy and a hollow system of justice, and this is why I think it is far too soon to say *Never Again* for my country.

We are not binding up the wounds of history. And I can assure you of this as a Rwandan: History dies hard.

I was not the only one who said no. There were thousands of other people in Rwanda who were also unimpressed by the propaganda and put their lives in jeopardy to shelter fugitives. Individual acts of courage happened every single day of the genocide. Some were partial killers, it is true, showing compassion to some and murdering others. But there were many who refused completely, and there would have been almost no survivors of the genocide without the thousands of secret kindnesses dispensed under the cover of night. We will never know the names of all those who opened their homes to hide would-be victims. Rwanda was full of ordinary killers, it is true, but it was also full of ordinary heroes.

There was a Muslim man, for example, who concealed up to thirty people in his sheds and outhouses. One of his guests reported the following: "The *Interahamwe* killer was chasing me down the alley. I was going to die any second. I banged on the door of the yard. It opened almost immediately. He took me by the hand and stood in his doorway and told the killer to leave. He said the Koran says if you save one life it is like saving the whole world. He did not know it is a Jewish text as well."

There was also Father Célestin Hakizimana, who presided over St. Paul's Pastoral Center in Kigali. He stood in contrast to those other priests and ministers who either condoned the genocide or slunk away when danger came. Father Hakizimana turned his church into a shelter for over two thousand people and refused to budge to the demands of the militia.

There was Damas Mutezintare Gisimba, who received four hundred hunted children into his orphanage. Many of them were hidden in chambers in the ceiling, along with prominent politicians. Gisimba also roamed around Kigali poking through the stacks of dead bodies piling up all around. He found several people not yet dead and took them into his care.

There were so many others. A farmer saved people by hiding them in trenches on his land and covering them up with plants and banana leaves to make it look like an ordinary field. An elderly woman pretended to be a sorceress and threatened to call down the power of the gods on any killers who tried to harm the people in her protection. A mayor used his own police force to fight the *Interahamwe* and was killed for his actions. Schoolteachers hid their hunted students in sheds and empty classrooms. Some of the names of these heroes are known, but most are not. Their good deeds are lost to history. The murders were anonymous and irrational, but the kindness and the bravery were there in scattered places too, and that is a big part of what gives me hope for the future.

What did these people have in common? I believe they all shared the long vision. They had an ability to see through the passing moment and to understand that the frenzy that had gripped Rwanda was a temporary condition at best. They acted decently, as was appropriate for decent times, and did not believe the world to be anything less than an essentially decent place, despite the onset of a collective insanity. Their body temperatures did not fluctuate with the changing environment. All these ordinary heroes believed that balance would one day be restored.

Let me explain a little more. The English scholar and

theologian C. S. Lewis was a veteran of the trenches of World War I and also the air blitz against London by the Nazis. He took note of a common delusion that comes in times of war: We have a tendency to believe that the horrors we are seeing are the unvarnished real state of mankind, an animal condition without a shred of true love or kindness to be found anywhere, a life of nasty, brutish shortness. Six thousand years of civilization somehow becomes nothing but a painted shell covering up an ugly "truth" about man.

Lewis described the attitude this way: "In hatred you see men as they are; you are disillusioned; but the loveliness of a loved person is merely a subjective haze concealing a 'real' core of sexual appetite or economic association. Wars and poverty are 'really' horrible; peace and plenty are mere physical facts about which men happen to have certain sentiments."

He disagreed with this view of reality, and I disagree as well. Kindness is not an illusion and violence is not a rule. The true resting state of human affairs is not represented by a man hacking his neighbor into pieces with a machete. That is a sick aberration. No, the true state of human affairs is life as it *ought to be lived.* Walk outside your door and this is almost certainly what you'll see all around you. Daily life in any culture consists of people working alongside each other, buying and selling from one another, laughing with each other, ignoring each other, showing each other courtesy, swearing at each other, loving each other, but hardly ever killing each other as a matter of routine. In the total scope of man's existence collective murder is a rare event and should never be considered the "real" fate of mankind.

I do not at all mean to downplay the role of politicized mass murder. It is a pathology of civilization and it will certainly happen again, probably before the decade is out. My point here is to say that it is not—and should never be seen as—the default state of mankind. These things are *not supposed to happen,* and when we write them off as Darwinist spectacles, inevitable by-products of war or worse, to ancient tribal animosities, we have lost sight of the most important thing: the fundamental perversion of genocide. We will have played into the hands of those who excite racial hatreds as a device to acquire more power. We will have been duped by the cheapest trick in the book. Human beings were designed to live sanely, and sanity *always* returns. The world always rights itself in the long run. Our collective biology simply refuses to let us go astray for long. Or as the French philosopher Albert Camus put it: "Happiness, too, is inevitable."

This is why I say that the individual's most potent weapon is a stubborn belief in the triumph of common decency. It is a simple belief, but it is not at all naive. It is, in fact, the shrewdest attitude possible. It is the best way to sabotage evil.

Let me tell you the most important thing I learned about evil.

Evil is a big, ugly, hulking creature. It is a formidable enemy in a frontal attack. But it is not very smart and not very fast. You can beat it if you can slip around its sides. Evil can be frustrated by people you might think are weaklings. Quiet, ordinary people are often the only people with the real ability to defeat evil. They can give it the *Rwandan no*.

I was a good-natured fellow with the guests who came into the hotel, no matter if they were good friends or odious hate mongers. This was in my nature. There are very few people with whom I could not sit and enjoy a glass of cognac. Except in extreme circumstances it very rarely pays to show hostility to the people in your orbit. And so when evil dropped by for a drink I was able to have a conversation. I could find its weaknesses and seek out its soft spots. I could see the vanity and the insecurity and even the ghost of common decency inside the minds of killers that would allow me to save lives. I could quietly flip evil's assets against itself. What happened at the Mille Collines was the most extreme form of pragmatism. We would go to any length and do whatever it took to save as many lives as possible. That was the basic ideology. That was the *only* ideology. There was nothing particularly special about this—it only seemed like the normal thing to do.

I looked into the abyss during the genocide, and the abyss looked back and we were able to reach a compromise that was actually no compromise at all. The swimming pool in which babies might have been drowned was turned into a village well.

Policemen who might have been directing death squads were instead posted at my front gate to help me keep out the killers. The hotel itself was supposed to have been a gathering place where refugees could be lured with false promises and then killed as a bunch. But it never happened. Tools of death became reappropriated. They were now tools of life.

I remember reading this in the Bible when I was a young man: "What is your life? You are a mist that appears for a little while and then vanishes." Our time here on the earth is short, and our chance to make a difference is tiny. For me the grinding blocks of history came together in such a way that I was able to take what fragile defense I had and hold it in place for seventy-six days. If I was able to give much it was only because I had some useful things from my life to give. I am a hotel manager, trained to negotiate contracts and provide shelter for those who need it. My job never changed, even in a sea of fire.

Wherever the killing season should next begin and people should become strangers to their neighbors and themselves, my hope is that there will still be those ordinary men who say a quiet no and open the rooms upstairs.

SELECTED BIBLIOGRAPHY

There have been several excellent accounts of the Rwandan genocide and the authors of this book did not hesitate to mine them for context and detail. These other works are gratefully acknowledged here.

The most rigorous and complete autopsy is *Leave None to Tell the Story: Genocide in Rwanda* by Alison Des Forges (New York: Human Rights Watch and International Federation of Human Rights, 1999). Des Forges and a team of researchers used Rwandan government documents from that period to produce a 771-page report of unparalleled authority. Philip Gourevitch's *We Wish to Inform You That Tomorrow We Will Be Killed with Our Families: Stories from Rwanda* (New York: Picador, 1998) is a work of distinguished reportage and unforgettable writing. *Shake Hands with the Devil: The Failure of Humanity in Rwanda* by Romeo Dallaire (New York: Avalon, 2004) is a cri de coeur that also happens to be a fine work of journalism. *Season of Blood: A Rwandan Journey* by Fergal Keane (London: Penguin Books, 1995) has a good section on

Rwanda's murky politics of ethnicity. *Machete Season: The Killers in Rwanda Speak* by Jean Hatzfeld, and translated by Linda Coverdale (New York: Farrar, Straus & Giroux, 2005) explores the motivations for mass murder from the most authoritative source possible: the killers themselves. Two quotes in the last chapter were drawn from Hatzfeld's impressive and troubling work.

Justice on the Grass: Three Rwandan Journalists, Their Trial for War Crimes, and a Nation's Quest for Redemption by Dina Temple-Raston (New York: Free Press, 2005) contains an excellent dissection of RTLM's role in inciting the massacres. A portion of a broadcast is quoted from Temple-Raston's work. The United Nations' report on the disaster, entitled "Report of the Independent Inquiry into the Actions of the United Nations During the 1994 Genocide in Rwanda," by a committee led by Ingvar Carlsson, Han Sung-Joo, and Rufus M. Kapolati and dated December 15, 1999, is a blunt condemnation of the various missteps in New York that cost the lives of approximately half a million people. *The Key to My Neighbor's House* by Elizabeth Neuffer (New York: Picador, 2001; London: Bloomsbury, 2001) asks penetrating questions about justice in the aftermath of genocide, and Samantha Power's *A Problem from Hell: America and the Age of Genocide* (New York: Basic Books, 2002; London: Flamingo, 2004) is an indictment of the West's tendency to fold in the face of evil. A memo from the U.S. State Department is drawn from Power's book. Some of the information about the forgotten heroes of 1994, as well as some colonial history, was drawn from materials at the excellent Gisozi Genocide Museum in Kigali.

Land of a Thousand Hills: My Life in Rwanda by Rosamond Halsey Carr with Ann Howard Halsey (New York: Viking Penguin, 1999; London: Viking/Allen Lane, 1999) is the autobiography of Mugongo's orphanage director, who is a treasure of Central Africa and a sharp observer of politics and people. Finally, Keir Pearson and Terry George's masterful screenplay for the movie *Hotel Rwanda,* reprinted in their book *Hotel Rwanda: Bringing the True Story of an African Hero to Film* (New York: Newmarket Press, 2005) ensured that the events at the Hotel Mille Collines would be known throughout the world.

A NOTE ON THE AUTHORS

Paul Rusesabagina was the manager of the Hotel
des Diplomats and later of the Hotel des Mille Collines
in Kigali, Rwanda, during the Rwandan genocide. He is
a recipient of the US Presidential Medal of Freedom and
the National Civil Rights Museum's 2005 Freedom Medal.
He left Rwanda in 1995 and now lives with
his family in Belgium.

Tom Zoellner is a freelance journalist and writer,
who has worked as a reporter for the *San Francisco
Chronicle*. He lives in New York.